LOOKING UP WHEN YOU FEEL DOWN

Based on
Ephesians
1-3

GENE A. GETZ

Regal Books

A Division of GL Publications
Ventura, California, U.S.A.

Rights for publishing this book in other languages are contracted by Gospel Litera-
ture International foundation (GLINT). GLINT also provides technical help for
the adaptation, translation, and publishing of Bible study resources and books in
more than 100 languages worldwide. For further information, contact GLINT,
Post Office Box 6688, Ventura, California 93006, U.S.A., or the publisher.

Published by Regal Books
A Division of GL Publications
Ventura, California 93006
Printed in U.S.A.

Library of Congress Cataloging in Publication Data

Getz, Gene A.
  Looking up when you feel down.

    1. Bible. N.T. Ephesians I-III—Commentaries.
2. Christian life—1960-   . I. Title.
BS2695.3.G47   1985   227'.5077   85-2041
ISBN 0-8307-1028-0

TABLE OF CONTENTS

LIST OF FIGURES

RENEWAL:
A BIBLICAL PERSPECTIVE

This study in Paul's letter to the Ephesians is another book in the Biblical Renewal Series. Renewal is the essence of dynamic Christianity and the basis on which Christians, both in a corporate or Body sense and as individual believers, can determine the will of God. Paul made this clear when he wrote to the Roman Christians—"be transformed by the renewing of your mind. Then," he continued, "you will be able to test and approve what God's will is" (Rom. 12:2). Here Paul is talking about renewal in both a personal and a corporate sense. In other words, Paul is asking these Christians as a Body of believers to develop the mind of Christ through corporate renewal.

Personal renewal will not happen as God intended it unless it happens in the context of corporate renewal. On the other hand, corporate renewal will not happen as God intended without personal renewal. Both are necessary.

The larger circle represents Church Renewal. This is the most comprehensive concept in the New Testament. However,

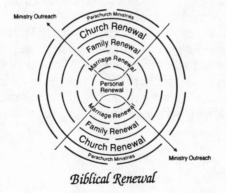

Biblical Renewal

every local *church* is made up of smaller self-contained, but interrelated units. The *family* in Scripture emerges as the church in miniature. In turn, the family is made up of an even smaller social unit—*marriage.* The third inner circle represents *personal* renewal, which is inseparably linked to all of the other basic units. Marriage is made up of two separate individuals who become one. The family is made up of parents and children who are also to reflect the mind of Christ. And the church is made up of not only individual Christians, but couples and families.

Though all of these social units are interrelated, biblical renewal can begin within any specific social unit. But wherever it begins—in the church, families, marriages or individuals—the process immediately touches all the other social units. And one thing is certain: All that God says is consistent and harmonious. He does not have one set of principles for the church and another set for the family, another for husbands and wives, and another for individual Christians. For example, the principles God outlines for local church elders, fathers and husbands, regarding their role as leaders, are interrelated and consistent. If they are not, we can be sure that we have not interpreted God's plan accurately.

Looking Up When You Feel Down is a study both in corporate and personal renewal. It begins with you as an individual Christian and demonstrates how you can grow spiritually in the context of a dynamic body of believers.

The Biblical Renewal Series is an expanding library of books by Gene Getz designed to provide supportive help in moving toward renewal. Each of these books fits into one of the circles described above and will provoke thought, provide interaction and tangible steps toward growth. You will find a detailed listing of the Biblical Renewal Series titles at the back of this book.

LOOKING UP WHEN
YOU FEEL DOWN

There is one thing we all have in common. There are times in our lives when we all feel down. It may be a brief period, or it may last for days or even weeks. There are a variety of reasons for these down periods.

The cause may be physical. We are tired. The demands of life may have left us exhausted.

The cause may be psychological. Stress has taken its toll. Or perhaps we are facing a natural result of a prolonged emotionally high experience.

The cause may also be spiritual. Perhaps we are living out of the will of God. Sin and guilt have gripped our minds and hearts.

Whatever the cause, there is a foundational solution. We must look beyond ourselves to the God who cares about us and loves us unconditionally—no matter what the source of our depression. Of course, if we are physically exhausted, we need rest. If we are psychologically drained, we need relief from pressure—and most of all an understanding and listening ear. And if we are living for ourselves, we need to focus on God and others. And in some instances we may need some professional assistance and help. But in all circumstances, we need to look up. There is Someone who cares more than any other person—pastor, doctor or counselor. That Someone is God our Father and our Saviour, Jesus Christ.

Paul's theme in Ephesians, chapters 1-3, focuses on a Christian's hope. In Christ we have been blessed in heavenly realms with every spiritual blessing (Eph. 1:3). The Holy Spirit who dwells in our hearts has guaranteed our eternal inheritance (1:14). In God's scheme of things we are already seated with Christ in the heavenly realms (2:6). But while on earth we are, with all Christians, a dwelling in which God lives by His Spirit (2:22). And until that day when we shall be with Christ, we have the potential to grow in our Christian lives and to be filled to the measure of the fulness of God (3:19).

So, if you are feeling down let Paul help you look up. Read and study this letter to the Ephesian Christians and be renewed and strengthened by a fresh understanding of your wonderful position in Jesus Christ.

1

Looking Up

EPHESIANS 1:1-2

Paul, an apostle of Christ Jesus by the will of God, to the saints in Ephesus, the faithful in Christ Jesus: Grace and peace to you from God our Father and the Lord Jesus Christ.

I remember the first time I stepped out the front door of the pension where my wife and I stayed in Innsbrook, Austria. After an opportunity to minister in Eastern Europe, we were able to spend a few days relaxing in this quaint Austrian city. In this one-time location of the Winter Olympics, I looked up to behold one of the most spectacular sights I've ever seen. Rising from the valley floor was a range of mountains occupying a segment of the Austrian landscape that nearly took my breath away. Many words can be used to describe those mountains—awesome, gorgeous, beautiful, inspiring.

I've been in mountain regions many times, but there was something unique and special about that experience in Innsbrook. For example, in the Colorado mountains, when you look up at a series of peaks, you may already be standing at 8,000 feet. But at Innsbrook, we were slightly above sea-level, looking straight up, nearly 8,000 feet. It was a breathtaking experience.

We know that all mountains are created by God and are beautiful and spectacular in their own right. But there are some that stand out above others. Just so, we also know that "all Scripture is God-breathed and is useful for teaching, rebuking, correcting and training in righteousness" (2 Tim. 3:16). But Ephesians stands out against the biblical landscape as one of the Holy Spirit's most lofty products of inspiration. Viewed and understood correctly, it too is spiritually breathtaking. In a relatively small section of the Bible, Paul takes us from earth to heaven as he unveils a Christian's wonderful and marvelous spiritual blessings in Christ. Someone has called this letter "the Switzerland of the New Testament."

GOD'S SPECIAL MESSENGER

"Paul, an apostle of Christ Jesus by the will of God" (Eph. 1:1).

Paul—the Author
Paul wrote this letter from a Roman prison, probably in A.D. 60 or 61 (4:1). Thus it is classified as one of the prison Epistles

along with Philemon, Philippians and Colossians. Perhaps this is one reason why the letter is so outstanding. In this semiprivate location he had more time to spend in quiet fellowship with the Holy Spirit. Though Paul was under custody in Rome, Luke reported that he was able to have his own rented home where he could freely receive visitors (Acts 28:30); nevertheless, he had more time to think, reflect, pray and write than when he was actively involved on his missionary tours.

Paul—an Apostle

As in most of his letters, Paul immediately identified himself as an apostle.[1] This is particularly appropriate in this Epistle because he later describes his special calling in Christ as an apostle to the Gentiles (Eph. 3:1-13).

An apostle was no ordinary person in the New Testament Church. It involved one of the "greater gifts" to the Body of Christ (1 Cor. 12:28). Later in this Ephesian letter Paul described apostleship along with prophetic ability as being foundational gifts (Eph. 2:20).

Don't misunderstand. Paul was not proud of his record, particularly as an unconverted Jew. Rather, to the Corinthians he stated: "For I am the least of the apostles and do not even deserve to be called an apostle, because I persecuted the church of God. But," he continued, "by the grace of God I am what I am" (1 Cor. 15:9-10).

Though few individuals were identified as apostles other than the original twelve, only Paul was ranked with those Jesus personally called and appointed to launch the Church.[2] His position was unique! And so was his calling. He, too, had a *direct* encounter with Jesus Christ.

Paul's Special Calling

Paul, whose original name was Saul, first appeared in the biblical record after the Church was founded at Jerusalem. Christians already numbered in the thousands.

The scene was dramatic and chilling. Stephen had just delivered a powerful witness before the Sanhedrin, a group of unbelieving Jews who were the primary leaders in Israel. His message was so penetrating and spiritually convicting that these men responded with threats and anger. "They were furious"— so much so that they "gnashed their teeth at him" (Acts 7:54). Their next move was to rush him, drag him out of the city and to stone him. And as they did, they "laid their clothes at the feet of a young man named Saul" who "was there, giving approval to his death" (7:58; 8:1).

From that day forward, Paul (Saul) led the persecution against Christians. His goal was to "destroy the church." Consequently, he went "from house to house" and "dragged off men and women and put them in prison" (8:3).

This angry young man was so intense and successful in his efforts that Christians could no longer stay in Jerusalem. They were scattered throughout the New Testament world (8:1). But Paul was not satisfied. He got permission from the high priest to go to Damascus to carry on his same murderous activities (9:1-2).

And then it happened! "As he neared Damascus on his journey, suddenly a light from heaven flashed around him. He fell to the ground and heard a voice say to him, 'Saul, Saul, why do you persecute me?'" (9:3-4).

The voice was that of Jesus Christ. Though struck blind, Paul was converted then and there. The Lord led him on to Damascus—but for a different purpose entirely. Paul the "persecutor" became the "persecuted." It was there he discovered he had a special mission in life; that he was God's chosen instrument to carry the message of Jesus Christ in a special way to the Gentile world (9:15). Ironically, he—now as a Christian—had to leave Damascus because of a conspiracy to take his life (9:23-25).

Paul never got over the grace that God extended to him that day on the Damascus road. The Lord could have struck him dead—not blind. Paul knew he deserved eternal separation from God. He had taken the lives of some of God's chosen people. Thus he wrote to Timothy, "Even though I was once a *blasphemer* and a *persecutor* and a *violent man,* I was shown mercy because I acted in ignorance and unbelief. The grace of our Lord was poured out on me abundantly, along with the faith and love that are in Christ Jesus" (1 Tim. 1:13-14).[3]

The apostle Paul knew by experience that God saves sinners. He classified himself as the "worst." But he also said, "For that very reason I was shown mercy so that in me, the *worst of sinners*, Christ Jesus might display his unlimited patience as an example for those who would believe on him and receive eternal life" (1:16). In other words, Paul knew that if God could save him, He could save anybody! Paul never forgot that reality. It was indelibly impressed upon his heart and affected the rest of his life. Thus he began his letter to the Ephesians, "Paul, an apostle of Christ Jesus by the will of God." He knew his calling was *divine*. To the Galatians, he made it even clearer, when he said, "Paul, an apostle—sent *not from men nor by man, but by Jesus Christ and God the Father*" (Gal. 1:1).

GOD'S FAITHFUL PEOPLE

There are some Bible interpreters who believe this letter to the Ephesians was designed by Paul to be a circular letter. This conclusion is based on several reasons. First, some of the earliest manuscripts omit references to the phrase "in Ephesus." Second, Paul omits any personal greeting in the letter. Third, the letter definitely treats a broad spectrum of teaching that does not relate to specific aspects of a particular local church. In fact, it is one of the few letters in which Paul deals extensively with the concept of the universal Church.

If these conclusions are true, it is also true that very early in the history of the Church, the Epistle was identified as having been written to the Ephesian Christians. My personal opinion is that the letter was designed by the Holy Spirit to be circular— that is, to be read in other churches in Asia—but that Paul probably had the Ephesians in mind when he wrote the Epistle. On the other hand, since he had a multiple purpose in mind, he wrote more generally so as not to restrict its use to one particular church.

The City of Ephesus

Ephesus was an important city in the New Testament world.

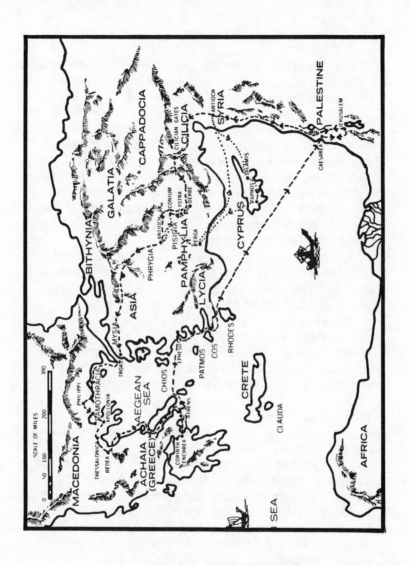

PAUL'S
FIRST AND SECOND
MISSIONARY JOURNEYS
Paul's first journey ·▷···▷·······
Paul's second journey ▷ ▷ ▷ ▬

Like the other great centers of population in the Roman culture, it was totally pagan. It was the capital of the province of Asia and was a great trading center. (See figure 2.)

Ephesus was also a great religious center, for the temple of Artemis was located there. This great temple was considered one of the Seven Wonders of the Ancient World. An annual festival was held in Artemis's honor during the months of March and April. People actually worshiped Artemis by means of sensual orgies and ceremonial prostitution. Fathers, mothers and children observed and took part in these degenerate activities. Multitudes of female virgins were continually initiated as "priestesses" to serve as temple prostitutes.

Ephesus also sported a huge open-air theater that seated up to 50,000 spectators. It was in this great coliseum that people gathered to watch various kinds of competitive athletic activities, as well as to see wild beasts fight to their death.

This great city was also the center of occult practice. Simpson and Bruce comment that "all manner of abominations, whether juggleries or positive works of the Devil, throve as in a hot house. It was in this deeply vitiated atmosphere, where sorcery or arts of crafty illusion tainted the very air."[4]

The Ephesian Christians

The message of Christ penetrated this pagan environment just as it had many other centers of idolatry. When Paul first came to Ephesus, he found a number of Jews who had already responded to the message of John the Baptist (Acts 19:1-3). However, they had not been taught the full gospel message. Paul began at that point, sharing with them that Jesus Christ had died, rose again and ascended to heaven, and that the Holy Spirit had come in His place. These people responded to this message and the Church was born in Ephesus (Acts 19:4-8).

Paul then began an aggressive evangelistic ministry. Initially he entered the Jewish synagogue attempting to persuade his fellow Jews that Jesus Christ was the true Messiah. But Luke records that "some of them became obstinate; they refused to believe and publicly maligned the Way" (19:9).

Paul then left the synagogue as his base of operation and

moved to "the lecture hall of Tyrannus." There he taught for two years, sharing the gospel with both Jews and Gentiles who would listen to his message. In fact, during this two-year period, men and women came from all over Asia to hear Paul speak (19:10). This perhaps helps explain why Paul later wrote a circular letter. Many people throughout Asia had become Christians while visiting Ephesus and had probably returned to start churches in their own communities.

Paul's ministry was so successful in Ephesus that it began to interfere with the idol business. Many people openly and publicly turned their back on occult practices. On one occasion, "a number who had practiced sorcery brought their scrolls together and burned them publicly" (19:19). Luke records that the value of the books totalled 50,000 drachmas. A drachma was about a day's wages. By today's standards, that could have been a $4-million or $5-million bonfire.

Most pagans are tolerant of others' religious beliefs—*until* it begins to affect their financial resources. And so it happened in Ephesus. Demetrius, a silversmith, had a thriving business making shrines of Artemis. But when great numbers of people turned their backs on idolatry—not only in Ephesus, but all over Asia—Demetrius got nervous. He called an emergency meeting, inviting his fellow craftsmen. "Men," he said, "you know we receive a good income from this business. And you see and hear how this fellow Paul has convinced and led astray large numbers of people here in Ephesus and in practically the whole province of Asia. He says that man-made gods are no gods at all" (19:25-26).

To add additional motivation, Demetrius decided to get religious. "There is a danger," he continued, "not only that our trade will lose its good name, but also that the temple of the great goddess Artemis will be discredited, and the goddess herself, who is worshiped throughout the province of Asia and the world, will be robbed of her divine majesty" (19:27).

Demetrius's final comments provided the fuel that fanned a smoldering "business concern" into a roaring fire. They turned an economic interest into a religious issue. They began shouting: "Great is Artemis of the Ephesians!" It wasn't long before the whole city joined in the chant! After hours of total confusion, the uproar subsided and, miraculously, Paul and his fellow workers were able to leave the city unharmed, leaving a band of people who had turned their backs on idolatry and witchcraft and become followers of Jesus Christ. These people Paul identified in his letter as "the *saints* in Ephesus, the *faithful* in Christ Jesus" (Eph. 1:1).

GOD'S GRACE TO YOU

There is a main thought that should invade our minds as we reflect on Paul's conversion on the Damascus Road, followed years later by those in Ephesus who also came to know Jesus Christ and personal forgiveness through Paul's ministry. The apostle said it well when he wrote to Timothy: "Here is a trustworthy thing that deserves full acceptance: Christ Jesus came into the world to save sinners—of whom I am the worst. But for that very reason I was shown mercy so that in me, the worst of sinners, Christ Jesus might display his unlimited patience as an example for those who would believe on him and receive eternal life" (1 Tim. 1:15-16).

The Ephesian Christians bore witness to the reality of Paul's confession. They worshiped idols and blended their worship with the worst kind of sexual immorality. Many had given themselves over to Satan and were controlled by demons. They, like Paul, were also the worst of sinners. Yet they experienced God's marvelous grace and forgiveness.

Note that Paul was religious in a different way. He actually worshiped the one true God, but initially rejected God's Son. Furthermore, he kept the law of Moses faithfully. Listen to his testimony as he wrote to the Philippians:

"If anyone else thinks he has reasons to put confidence in the flesh, I have more:
- circumcised on the eighth day,
- of the people of Israel,
- of the tribe of Benjamin,
- a Hebrew of Hebrews;
- in regard to the law, a Pharisee;

• as for zeal, persecuting the church;
• as for legalistic righteousness, faultless" (Phil. 3:4-6).

On the other hand, the Ephesians represent the other end of the continuum. They were without God in this world, separated from the promises made to Israel. They were totally pagan—though religious.

But God's amazing grace has been extended to both the Jews and Gentiles. In many respects this is one of Paul's major themes in the Ephesian letter. Furthermore, it does not matter how deep we have sunk in sin's mire. The experiences of both Paul and the Ephesian Christians illustrate this point. And throughout history this reality has been verified again and again.

John Newton serves as a classic illustration. Richard Sume tells the story dramatically in his unpublished manuscript entitled "The Eye of the Storm." He writes:

> From the records preserved and passed down to us, young John lost his mother when he was but seven years old. She was the one guiding light in his early life. At eleven he went to sea—off to Africa that he might be free to sin to his heart's content. During the next few years his soul was seared by some of the most revolting and barbarous human experiences and became involved in the unspeakable atrocities of the African slave trade. During those days, he was actually sold to a black woman who made him depend upon her for his meager food. To use his own words here, he became a slave of slaves.
>
> And then it happened. It took place on the tenth of March, 1748, on board a ship that was threatening to flounder in the grip of a storm. "That tenth of March," wrote Newton, "is a day much to be remembered by me and I've not suffered it to pass unnoticed since the year 1748. For on that day, March 10, 1748, the Lord came from on high and delivered me out of deep waters." As the ship plunged down into the trough of the sea, few on

board expected her to come up again. The hold was rapidly filling with water. As Newton rushed to his place at the pumps, he said to the captain, "If this will not do, Lord have mercy upon us." His own words startled him. "Mercy?" he said to himself in astonishment. "Mercy? What mercy can there be for me? This was the first desire I've breathed for mercy in many years. About 6:00 in the evening the hold was free from water and then came a gleam of hope. I thought I saw the hand of God displayed in our favor. I began to pray. My prayer for mercy was like the cry of the ravens which yet the Lord Jesus does not disdain to hear."

In concluding the story of his conversion, Newton says, "In the gospel I saw at least a ray of hope. But on every other side I was surrounded by black unfathomable despair." On that ray of hope, Newton staked everything and on the tenth of March, 1748, he sought mercy and found it. Is it any wonder? Is it any surprise that out of that experience Newton has given the church of God perhaps its finest hymn on the grace of God that redeems:

Amazing grace! how sweet the sound,
That saved a wretch like me!
I once was lost, but now am found,
Was blind, but now I see.

'Twas grace that taught my heart to fear,
And grace my fears relieved;
How precious did that grace appear
The hour I first believed!

Thru many dangers, toils and snares,
I have already come;
'Tis grace hath brought me safe thus far,
And grace will lead me home.

John Newton, like Paul, like the Ephesians and like all of us who are Christians, illustrated the amazing grace of God. His tombstone bears this inscription:

> John Newton, Clerk; once an infidel and libertine, a servant of slaves in Africa, was by the rich mercy of our Lord and Saviour Jesus Christ preserved, restored, pardoned, and appointed to preach the faith he had long laboured to destroy.

WHAT ABOUT YOU?

Do you feel God would never accept you? Take heart. He accepted the Ephesians. He accepted Paul. He accepted John Newton. He'll accept you—no matter what your sin. The blood of Jesus Christ cleanses from all sin.

Or perhaps you're like Paul. You try to keep the Ten Commandments. You've even taken a stand against what you believe is wrong. Yet, you've never accepted Jesus Christ as your personal Saviour. Remember that after describing both the Jew and the Gentile in his letter to the Romans, Paul summarized his thoughts with this statement: "For all have sinned and fall short of the glory of God" (Rom. 3:23). No matter what our background—good or bad—we all need to receive Jesus Christ for forgiveness of sin.

A PRAYER OF ACCEPTANCE

"Dear Father, I acknowledge that I have sinned and come short of God's glory. I recognize that the wages of my sin are death. But I thank you that even though I am a sinner, Christ died for me. I thank you that by faith in His death and resurrection I can be justified and made righteous and have peace with you through the Lord Jesus Christ. This moment I receive you as my personal Saviour. Thank you for coming into my life. Thank you for making me a Christian. This I pray in Jesus' name. Amen."

Notes

1. See Romans 1:1; 1 Corinthians 1:1; 2 Corinthians 1:1; Galatians 1:1; Colossians 1:1; 1 Timothy 1:1; Titus 1:1.
2. Matthias was chosen by lot to replace Judas (Acts 1:23-26).
3. Hereafter, all italicized words and phrases in Scripture quotations are added by the author for emphasis and clarification.
4. E. K. Simpson and F. F. Bruce, *Commentary on the Epistles to the Ephesians and Colossians* (Grand Rapids: Wm. B. Eerdmans Publishing Co., 1957), p. 17. Used by permission.

2

Looking Up
To God The Father

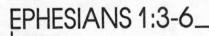

EPHESIANS 1:3-6

Praise be to the God and Father of our Lord Jesus Christ, who has blessed us in the heavenly realms with every spiritual blessing in Christ. For he chose us in him before the creation of the world to be holy and blameless in his sight. In love he predestined us to be adopted as his sons through Jesus Christ, in accordance with his pleasure and will—to the praise of his glorious grace, which he has freely given us in the One he loves.

Predictably, man's first explorations of outer space precipitated some interesting comments regarding the existence of God. For example, as soon as Russia's first satellite entered space, Moscow's magazine *Krokidil* indicated that "creation, from a communist point of view, is at last under new management." And later, the Russian astronaut Gherman Titoy said after his return from space: "Some people say there is a God out there . . . . But in my travels around the earth all day long, I looked around and didn't see Him . . . . I saw no God or angels. The rocket was made by our own people. I don't believe in God. I believe in man, his strength, his possibilities, his reason."

By contrast, astronaut John Glenn, on one occasion delivered a sermon entitled "Why I Know There Is a God." It was delivered on Layman's Sunday in an Arlington, Virginia church. It was a message in simple terms in belief in God and in Christian principles. He concluded with the thought that man is placed on earth as a free agent. He is given freedom of choice and only he can make the decision as to whether he will or will not live by the guidelines which Christ followed throughout His days on earth.

On another occasion, astronaut James A. McDivitt, who orbited the earth 62 times with Edward H. White II aboard Gemini IV said in a talk in a foreign press club in Rome: "I did not see God looking into my space-cabin window, as I do not see God looking into my car's windshield on earth. But I could recognize His work in the stars as well as when walking among flowers in a garden. If you can be with God on earth, you can be with God in space as well."

King David put all of these thoughts in proper perspective when he said, "The fool says in his heart, 'There is no God'" (Ps. 14:1). Why is this true? Again David has spoken clearly: "The heavens declare the glory of God; the skies proclaim the work of his hands" (Ps. 19:1).

Another psalmist personalized David's words. He knew where to look for guidance and encouragement, particularly in a time of deep need. Thus he wrote: "I lift up my eyes to the hills—where does my help come from? My help comes from the Lord, the Maker of heaven and earth" (Ps. 121:1-2).

Paul in his letter to the Ephesians helps every Christian

focus on God as the source of grace and power. So if you're feeling down, look up! As you read this chapter, lift up your eyes with the psalmist of old.

PRAISE TO THE THREE-IN-ONE

After extending "grace and peace" to the Ephesian Christians from God the Father and the Lord Jesus Christ (1:2), Paul launched into a grand statement of praise and adoration that ends up being one elongated sentence from verse 3 to verse 14. It is no doubt the longest sentence in the Bible. This, of course, is not discernible in our English versions since the translators have added normal punctuation to help us follow the flow of Paul's thoughts.

Since Paul's ideas in this letter appear to be somewhat overlapping and interwoven, it is not as easy to analyze and present what he said in his opening section of the Ephesian letter in a logical and systematic way. Perhaps Paul's very writing style is somewhat symbolic of the truth he presents. Throughout church history theologians have tried to explain, in a logical and systematic way, what Paul teaches here. Unfortunately, they always end up, if they're honest with themselves, admitting that there is no way to totally and logically explain all that Paul is teaching. We end up with what some call a biblical paradox. Personally, I like the word *antinomy* better. Here Paul focuses on two basic antinomies—the Trinity and God's sovereignty as it relates to free will.

However, there *is* order and sequence in what Paul wrote. In spite of this one-sentence paragraph which covers 12 verses in our English translations, there are three natural divisions.

In verses 3 to 6, Paul focused on *God the Father*.

In verses 7 to 12 he focused on *God the Son*.

In verses 13 and 14, he focused on *God the Holy Spirit*.

Furthermore, he concluded each division with a three-fold refrain:

- "to the *praise of his glorious grace,* which he has freely given us in the one he loves" (1:6)

- "in order that we, who were the first to hope in Christ, might be for the *praise of his glory*" *(1:12)*
- "*who is a deposit guaranteeing our inheritance until the redemption of those who are God's possession—to the praise of his glory*" (1:14).

All that Paul shared is related to God's plan of salvation for lost humanity.

God the Father *planned* it.

Jesus Christ *executed* God's plan.

The Holy Spirit has *guaranteed* that the plan would be ultimately culminated.

In this paragraph Paul takes us from eternity into time, and back again to eternity. And one thing is clear! God is all in all.

GOD THE FATHER

God's Actions

In this letter Paul stated God's blessing towards those who know Christ in two ways:

He chose us

First, He chose us in Christ before the creation of the world (1:4). Our salvation was not an afterthought with God. We were in His mind and heart before He created any part of this world.

He adopted us

Second, He predestined us (that is, "marked out beforehand") "*to be adopted as his sons*" (1:5). As believers in Jesus Christ we are God's children. He is our heavenly Father. Together, all believers are brothers and sisters in Christ—members of God's eternal family.

A Believer's Benefits

As Christians, our benefits of knowing these truths are also two-fold:

We have eternal life

First, and most important, we have eternal life. We have *hope.* We have security for the future. Paul, writing to the Romans, clarified this reality. He posed a question with a series of questions. "What, then, shall we say in response to this?" (Rom. 8:31).

Paul here was referring to the same truth he had shared with the Ephesians and which he had summarized to the Romans in the two previous verses: "For those God foreknew he also *predestined* to be conformed to the likeness of his Son, that he might be the firstborn among many brothers. And those he predestined, he also *called;* those he called, he also *justified;* those he justified, he also *glorified*" (8:29-30).

Since our salvation has been planned by God, executed by the Son of God and sealed by the Holy Spirit, "what then shall we say in response to this?" The following is Paul's answer, with a series of questions:

- "If God is for us, who can be against us?" (8:31).
- "He who did not spare his own Son, but gave him up for us all—how will he not also, along with him, graciously give us all things?" (8:32).
- "Who will bring any charge against those whom God has chosen?" ("It is God who justifies") (8:33).
- "Who is he that condemns?" ("Christ Jesus, who died—more than that, who was raised to life—is at the right hand of God and is also interceding for us") (8:34).
- "Who shall separate us from the love of Christ?" (8:35).
- "Shall trouble or hardship or persecution or famine or nakedness or danger or sword?" (8:35).

Paul's *answer* to this series of questions is straightforward and to the point:

"No, in all these things we are more than conquerors through him who loved us. For I am convinced that
- neither death nor life,
- neither angels nor demons,
- neither the present nor the future,
- nor any powers,

- neither height nor depth,
- nor anything else in all creation,

will be able to separate us from the love of God that is in Christ Jesus our Lord" (8:37-39).

Why did Paul share these great truths in his letters to the Ephesians and the Romans? The answer is clear: It's that we might have a sense of security and hope. For several years in my own Christian life, I did not have this sense of hope. True, I was a Christian, but I was trying to keep myself saved in my own strength, by what I did. My security was based on feelings and emotions. Consequently, I was a "roller-coaster" Christian. My life was generally quite miserable.

To this very day I can go back to those same Christians I grew up with and ask them if they are saved. Their response is always tentative. "We really can't know for sure," is their response. "But, if I'm true and faithful, maybe God will be merciful."

Dear friend, God has already been merciful! If we are truly saved, if we truly know Jesus Christ, our salvation is sealed— now and eternally. And God wants us to have a sense of security. Thus John wrote, "I write these things to you who believe in the name of the Son of God so that *you may know* that you have eternal life" (1 John 5:13).

We are under God's control

The second benefit of knowing these truths is that our lives in this world are also under God's sovereign control. Nothing happens by accident. Paul also made this point clear in the same passage in his letter to the Romans when he wrote, "And we know that in *all things* God works for the good of those who love him, who have been called according to his purpose" (Rom. 8:28).

Though difficult to accept and understand, especially in the midst of crisis situations, it is true nevertheless, that God is in control. Job illustrates this more than any other biblical personality. He could not understand the calamities that came into his life. Even his wife eventually told him to curse God and die.

Job's response was amazing and reflected a theology that

recognized the sovereignty of God. He reported that he would trust God even though He took his life (Job 13:15). Job was able to see beyond his human predicament to the God who is just and is ultimately in control of all things. He kept looking up when he felt horribly down!

Joseph stands out as another classic Old Testament illustration. Even though unjustly criticized by his brothers, mercilessly sold as a slave, falsely accused of sexual immorality and then ruthlessly thrown into prison as an innocent man, his response to his brothers years later flashes like a huge neon sign down through the centuries for all to see: "You intended to harm me," he said to his brothers, "but God intended it for good to accomplish what is now being done, the saving of many lives" (Gen. 50:20).

Though Joseph was terribly mistreated, there was no sign of anger, bitterness, nor desire to retaliate and take vengeance on those who hurt him. Only a proper view of God enabled this man to respond as he did.

A Proper Response

How should a Christian respond to the truth Paul wrote about in this opening section of his Ephesian letter? Our response should also be two-fold:

First, we should praise and glorify God, particularly when we are facing difficult challenges and find ourselves in trying circumstances. While Paul was chained to a Roman guard, he wrote, "Praise be to the God and Father of our Lord Jesus Christ, who has blessed us in the heavenly realms with every spiritual blessing in Christ" (Eph. 1:3).

Most Christians need a clearer understanding of God. We need to understand that at the very heart of the biblical revelation itself is a doctrine of God. Dr. George Peters states this fact beautifully:

> The Scriptures are emphatically theocentric in considering the universe; history of humankind; and the nature, life and purpose of man. Clearly the word states that all things are from Him, and through Him

and to Him and in the end God will be all in all (Rom.
11:36; 1 Cor. 15:28). Only a theocentric perspective
of the Bible gives us the right direction and can save
us from humanism in any form . . . .

God is and remains the final cause and source, the
supreme initiator and actor, and the ultimate perspective and goal of all existence, being, events and
processes. That majestic first statement in the Bible
'in the beginning'—reminds us that God is and
remains the fundamental and ultimate basis of all that
is and comes to pass . . . . God is God and not man.[1]

This was Paul's view of God when he penned the opening
sentences in his Ephesian letter. And because it was, it began
with concept of praise.

Second, we should "live a life worthy" of this high and heav-
enly calling (Eph. 4:1). This, of course, is where Paul was
headed in this letter. But he states it clearly right from the
beginning when he wrote, "For he chose us in him before the
creation of the world to be holy and blameless in his sight" (1:4).

Some day we will be with God and ultimately conformed into
the image of Jesus Christ. But it was never God's intention for
us to wait until then to begin living a holy and righteous life. Paul
made this point very clear in his letter to Titus when he wrote,
"For the grace of God that brings salvation has appeared to all
men" and "it teaches us to say 'No' to ungodliness and worldly
passions, and to live self-controlled, upright and godly lives in
this present age" (Titus 2:11-12). This, of course, is what Paul
was talking about in the opening part of the Ephesian letter. He
made it even clearer in chapter 2 when he wrote, "For it is by
grace you have been saved, through faith—and this not from
yourselves, it is the gift of God—not by works, so that no one
can boast. For we are God's workmanship, created in Christ
Jesus to do good works, which God prepared in advance for us
to do" (Eph. 2:8-9).

A proper view of God's grace leads to righteousness—not
unrighteousness. To be eternally secure in Christ should lead a

Christian to present his body a living and holy sacrifice to God (Rom. 12:1). To do less is to spurn God's love, to reject the One who gave everything.

Suppose you adopted a son into your home. You gave the child love, cared for his needs and nurtured him into adulthood. At a particular point in time you then turned the family business over to him. And then it happened! The moment the papers were signed and sealed, the son you adopted and loved so dearly suddenly told you he didn't want to talk to you ever again. He refused to answer the phone when you called. Your letters returned unopened. He went out of the way to avoid coming into your presence. Furthermore, he refused to associate with the rest of your family and friends.

How would you feel? The point, I think, is clear. God feels that way often about His adopted sons and daughters who spurn His grace and live for themselves. But wonder of wonders, He never stops loving us.

WHAT ABOUT GOD'S SOVEREIGNTY AND MAN'S FREE WILL?

There are some who approach a passage such as Paul wrote to the Ephesians and suddenly get bogged down in a theological quagmire. Questions flood their minds—legitimate questions, I might add.

If God chose us in Christ before the foundation of the world, how can I be free to choose?

What good is it to tell others they can be saved if we don't know whom God has chosen?

First of all we must realize that the Bible teaches that all men are free to accept or reject the message of salvation. Jesus Christ died for the whole world (John 3:16). Whoever will may come.

We cannot explain these two biblical realities. As Ken Boa states, "In some inexplicable way, God has seen fit to incorporate human freedom and responsibility into His all-inclusive plan. Even though the Lord is in sovereign control of the details in His creation, He never forces any man to do anything against His will."[2]

Here we can take a lesson from Paul. As F. Foulkes states: "This doctrine of election, or predestination, is not raised as a subject of controversy or speculation. It is not set in opposition to the self-evident fact of the free will of man. It involves a paradox that the New Testament does not seek to resolve, and that our finite minds cannot fathom. Paul emphasizes both the sovereign purpose of God and man's free will. He took the gospel of grace and offered it to all. Then to those who had accepted the gospel, he set forth the doctrine of election."[3]

Throughout church history, many men and women have tried to explain this biblical paradox—or antinomy. They cannot. No one has ever been successful. Unfortunately, they form two camps, leading to a division within the Body of Christ. And at times, if it weren't so tragic, it would be amusing.

The story is told of a group of theologians who were discussing predestination and free will. The argument grew so heated that sides were drawn and the group broke up into two fiercely prejudiced factions.

But one theologian, not knowing to which camp he belonged, stood for a moment trying to decide. At last he made up his mind to join in with the predestination crowd.

When he tried to push his way in, they asked, "Who sent you here?"

"Nobody sent me," he replied. "I came on my on free will."

"Free will?" they shouted at him. "You can't come in here of your own free will. You belong with the other group."

So he turned and went toward the free-will group.

When he tried to join them, someone asked, "When did you decide to join us?"

"I didn't decide. I was sent here," he answered.

"Sent here!" They were horrified. "You can't join us unless you choose to by your own free will." And so he was excluded from both companies.

Many Christians miss the marvelous part of Paul's opening thoughts in Ephesians when they allow themselves to get bogged down trying to *explain* God and His sovereignty. His thoughts begin where ours end. But there is one thing we can believe and accept—even though we don't understand it all— and allow it to transform our lives. It's this: "He chose us in him before the creation of the world to be holy and blameless in his sight. In love he predestined us to be adopted as his sons through Jesus Christ, in accordance with his pleasure and will— to the praise of his glorious grace, which he has freely given us in the One he loves" (Eph. 1:4-6).

Notes

1. Taken from A THEOLOGY OF CHURCH GROWTH, by George W. Peters. Copyright © 1981 by The Zondervan Corporation. Used by permission.
2. Kenneth Boa, *God I Don't Understand* (Wheaton: Victor Books, 1975), p. 51. Used by permission.
3. F. Foulkes, *The Epistle of Paul to the Ephesians* (Grand Rapids: Wm. B. Eerdmans Publishing Co., 1963), p. 46. Used by permission.

3

Looking Up
To God The Son

EPHESIANS 1:7-12

In him we have redemption through his blood, the forgiveness of sins, in accordance with the riches of God's grace that he lavished on us with all wisdom and understanding. And he made known to us the mystery of his will according to his good pleasure, which he purposed in Christ, to be put into effect when the times will have reached their fulfillment—to bring all things in heaven and on earth together under one head, even Christ.

In him we were also chosen, having been predestined according to the plan of him who works out everything in conformity with the purpose of his will, in order that we, who were the first to hope in Christ, might be for the praise of his glory.

One day Max Walsh left the warm environment of a mountain lodge in the Austrian Alps. The weather was clement and "friendly." But, as can happen in high altitudes, the weather changed suddenly and dramatically. Max found himself in a blinding snowstorm. Losing all sense of direction, he finally succumbed to the elements and collapsed.

The owner of the lodge, knowing the man had no doubt lost his way, sent his best dog to look for Walsh. Following his God-created instincts, the well-trained dog soon discovered Max, still lying where he had fallen and in a semiconscious state. Responding to his master's orders, the dog grabbed the sleeve of Walsh's frozen jacket and began to jerk and pull. Responding, Walsh began to regain his senses, saw the dog but mistook him for a wolf. Fear gripped him! Pulling his hunting knife from his sheath, he managed to reach out and stab his would-be savior.

Badly wounded, the dog let go and limped back to the lodge, where he fell dead at his master's feet. Sensing immediately what had happened, the owner of the lodge made his way through the blizzard, carefully following the trail of blood. He found Walsh, once again in a semiconscious state, but was able to carry him back to the safety of the lodge where he survived. Walsh's life was saved because a faithful dog carried out his master's command, literally shedding his blood in the process.

Many of us can listen to a story like this and be moved to tears. I remember as a young boy seeing the original movie, *Lassie, Come Home,* and cried my way through the film. When my son was about 10 years old we saw *Where the Red Fern Grows,* a story about two beautiful hunting dogs. One gave his life protecting his young master from a vicious attack by a mountain lion. Eventually, the other dog died of a broken heart, grieving over the loss of her faithful companion. Both my son and I sat and wept. It was a touching story!

As I reflected on these personal experiences, I couldn't help but wonder why we are so emotionally moved by dog stories such as these and yet so unmoved at times by the story of the One who shed His blood that we might live. I'm speaking, of course, of Jesus Christ the Son of God.

The Apostle Paul developed this theme in the Ephesian letter. As we've seen, God the Father planned our salvation (Eph. 1:3-6). In the verses before us in this chapter, we see that Jesus Christ, God's Son, was the One who executed God's plan. My purpose in this chapter is to help you look up to the cross to behold the Saviour of the world. But more important, I trust you'll look beyond the cross to the resurrected Christ who is seated in the heavenlies at the right hand of God.

CHRIST'S ACTIONS

Though verses 7 to 10 bring the work of Christ into sharp focus, the Son of God's part in our salvation appears throughout this introductory section.

- Jesus Christ is the means whereby we receive God's spiritual blessings (1:3).
- God chose us in Christ before He actually created the world (1:4).
- We were adopted as God's children through Jesus Christ (1:5).
- His glorious grace was freely given us "in the One He loves"—none other than Jesus Christ (1:6).

Paul next spoke of the specific action taken by Christ to make our salvation possible. He shed His blood on Calvary's cross. Thus Paul wrote: "In him we have redemption through his blood, the forgiveness of sins, in accordance with the riches of God's grace that he lavished on us with all wisdom and understanding" (1:7-8).

There are those who hear the message of the cross and respond with antagonism. In fact, some so-called scholars, scientists and even theologians have referred to the message of the Bible as a "slaughterhouse religion." In their pride and arrogance, they believe they have progressed beyond what they identify as a primitive approach to spiritual truth.

The facts are that if we remove the blood of Christ from the Bible, we have destroyed its central message. We are left with a library of books with hundreds of missing pages. And the content on the pages that remain lose all meaning and significance.

Why did God choose to save us through the shedding of blood? No human being can answer that question satisfactorily.

It is a unique and divine mystery, known only to God Himself. Someday, the reason will be clearer when we fellowship with the Son of God face to face. Until then, we must accept, believe and rejoice in God's statement that "without the shedding of blood there is no forgiveness" (Heb. 9:22). The New Testament writers affirm this truth again and again:

- Be shepherds of the church of God, which he bought with his own *blood*" (Acts 20:28).
- "For all have sinned and fall short of the glory of God, and are justified freely by his grace through the redemption that came by Christ Jesus. God presented him as a sacrifice of atonement, through faith in his *blood*" (Rom. 3:23-24).
- "Since we have now been justified by his *blood*, how much more shall we be saved from God's wrath through him!" (5:9).
- "In the same way, after supper he took the cup saying, 'This cup is the new covenant in my *blood*; do this, whenever you drink it, in remembrance of me'" (1 Cor. 11:25).
- "But now in Christ Jesus you who once were far away have been brought near through the *blood* of Christ" (Eph. 2:13).
- "For God was pleased to have all his fullness dwell in him, and through him to reconcile to himself all things, whether things on earth or things in heaven, by making peace through his *blood*, shed on the cross" (Col. 1:19-20).
- "Who have been chosen according to the foreknowledge of God the Father, by the sanctifying work of the Spirit, for obedience to Jesus Christ and sprinkling by his *blood*" (1 Pet. 1:2).
- "For you know that it was not with perishable things such as silver or gold that you were redeemed from the empty way of life handed down to you from your forefathers, but with the precious *blood* of Christ, a lamb without blemish or defect" (1:18-19).
- "If we walk in the light, as he is in the light, we have fellowship with one another, and the *blood* of Jesus, his Son, purifies us from every sin" (1 John 1:7).
- "To him who loves us and has freed us from our sins by his *blood*, and has made us to be a kingdom and priests to serve his God and Father—to him be glory and power forever and ever!" (Rev. 1:5-6).

These verses set the stage for our next major point in this lesson. What are the benefits that come to every Christian because Jesus Christ shed his blood on the cross?

A BELIEVER'S BENEFITS

Note how frequently the concept of "redemption" and "forgiveness" appear in the verses we've just outlined. Just so, Paul referred to these benefits in his Ephesian letter, in Jesus Christ we "have *redemption* through his blood, the *forgiveness* of sins" (Eph. 1:7).

Redemption

The concept of being "redeemed" has its roots in the Old Testament. Its basic meaning has to do with being released from the state of servitude because someone paid the price for our ransom.

Consider Israel! God's people were slaves in Egypt. This bondage continued approximately 400 years—and then God set them free. He "redeemed" His people. Ironically, the price that was paid involved those who were inflicting this bondage on these Israelites. "Every firstborn son in Egypt" had to die—including the "firstborn of the cattle as well" (Exod. 11:5).

But the most graphic illustration of redemption involved Israel's protection. In order to be delivered from the plague that took the life of every firstborn in Israel, God instructed His people to select a lamb, free from any defect. They were to slaughter this animal and have a special meal called "the Lord's Passover" (12:11). However, they were "to take some of the *blood* and put it on the sides and tops of the doorframes of the houses" where they had eaten the lambs (12:7). Moses has recorded the Lord's specific words: "On that same night I will pass through Egypt and strike down every firstborn—both men and animals—and I will bring judgment on all the gods of Egypt; I am the Lord. The *blood* will be a sign for you on the houses where you are; and when I see the *blood*, I will pass over you. No destructive plague will touch you when I strike Egypt" (12:12-13).

This Old Testament event is a graphic picture of Christ's redemptive work that Paul and other New Testament writers describe so frequently. This event, and later the whole sacrificial system set up in the Old Testament, pointed to the shed blood of Jesus Christ. John the Baptist recognized this truth when he first encountered Jesus Christ. We read that "the next day John saw Jesus coming toward him and said, 'Look, the *Lamb of God,* who takes away the sin of the world!'" (John 1:29).

The New Testament letter to the Hebrews made this point crystal clear. We read that when Jesus Christ came, "He entered the Most Holy Place once for all by his own *blood,* having obtained eternal redemption." The Old Testament priest entered "by means of the blood of goats and bulls." Not so our Lord Jesus Christ! He was our great High Priest and gave His life that we might live (Heb. 9:11-14).

Forgiveness

When Christ paid the price that could set mankind free from sin's bondage, it involved a very complex and comprehensive truth—forgiveness. Divine "forgiveness" and "redemption" are hand-in-glove concepts. That is why most biblical writers often include these realities in the same context, as Paul did in Ephesians.

To be forgiven by God means that God no longer holds our sins against us. The blood of Christ has paid the price for *all* sin—past, present, and future. And when we become believers, the blood of Christ keeps on cleansing us from sin. If it did not, we would not have eternal salvation, for as Christians we are not perfect. If it were not for Christ's finished work on the cross, the smallest sin would result in eternal separation from God.

What happens, then, when a believer sins? The Bible teaches that we will be *disciplined* by the Lord, but never *condemned* with the world (1 Cor. 11:31-32). When we confess our sins, we are restored to fellowship (1 John 1:9).

Substitution

Christ became a substitute for us. He died in our place. As Paul stated in his letter to the Corinthians—"God made him who had no sin to be sin for us, so that in him we might become the righteousness of God" (2 Cor. 5:21). Throughout the Old Testament it is clear that the whole concept of sacrifice for sins involves "substitution" which has been fulfilled in Christ. Peter stated: "He Himself bore our sins in his body on the tree, so that we might die to sins and live for righteousness; by his wounds you have been healed" (1 Pet. 2:24).

Throughout history we have some dramatic illustrations that help us as human beings understand in a very limited way what the substitutionary death of Jesus Christ actually means. For example, one such illustration took place during World War II.

Auschwitz was the first German concentration camp to become a place of extermination. The gas chambers were in constant use. Because of the great influx of new prisoners daily, the Germans also began to use firing squads.

One day the commandant selected 10 men from one barrack to be executed by the merciless firing squad. One of those selected was the father of a large family. When he was pulled from his place in line, he fell to the ground, begging for mercy. The Nazi official was unresponsive until the man standing next to the one on the ground, a Catholic priest named Maximillian Colbe, stepped forward to offer his life in exchange for the man on his knees. Surprisingly, the commandant agreed to such an arrangement. But instead of being led away to the firing squad, Father Maximillian was thrown into a tiny, damp cell where he suffered the agonizing death of starvation. Today, Maximillian Colbe is honored by millions of people because he died in the place of one man.

Jesus Christ, the sinless Son of God, through an agonizing death on the cross, died not for one man or a few or even several. He died for *all* human beings who have ever lived and who will ever live. I am deeply moved, as I'm sure you are, by the sacrificial and unselfish love that men like Maximillian Colbe demonstrate towards their fellow human beings. How much more should we be moved by the love of Jesus Christ for all mankind!

A PROPER RESPONSE

How should a Christian respond to such love—to "the riches of God's grace that he lavished on us with all wisdom and understanding" (Eph. 1:7-8)?

- How should God's children respond to the fact that God has "made known to us the mystery of his will according to his good pleasure, which he purposed in Christ" (1:9)?
- How should we respond as those who have been a part of God's great plan which He has "put into effect" (1:10)?
- How should we respond to the fact that "we are also chosen, having been predestined according to the plan of him who works out everything in conformity with the purpose of his will" (1:11)?

Paul answered these questions just as he did in culminating the earlier section in this letter that focused on God the Father. Our lives right now are to be lived in such a way that we *"might be for the praise of his glory"* (1:12). Not only should we lift our hearts and voices in praise to God, but our very lives should point to our glorious Lord Jesus Christ.

A PERSONAL RESPONSE

When we truly understand the love of Christ in providing redemption and forgiveness, it cannot help but impact our lives, both in relationship to God and others. Consider these questions.

Have I responded to Christ's provision and accepted His free gift of eternal life?

Remember, this gift is available to all. Jesus Christ died for the whole world. The Scriptures state: "For there is no difference between Jew and Gentile—the same Lord is Lord of all and richly blesses all who call on him, for, 'Everyone who calls on the name of the Lord will be saved'" (Rom. 10:12-13).

Have you forgiven others who have sinned against you?

This is a very practical application for every Christian. Christ is not only our Saviour from sin, but our example in the area of human forgiveness. Listen to the words of Paul: "Bear with each other and forgive whatever grievance you may have against one another. *Forgive as the Lord forgave you.* And over all these virtues put on love, which binds them all together in perfect unity" (Col. 3:13-14).

How has Christ's love for me affected my service for God?

Again, listen to the words of Paul: "Therefore, I urge you, brothers, in view of God's mercy, to offer your bodies as living sacrifices, holy and pleasing to God—which is your spiritual worship" (Rom. 12:1).

These questions, and particularly the third one, can be dramatically answered by a very unusual story that unfolded many years ago over a rather lengthy period of time. The story was born in an artist's studio in the city of Dusseldorf, Germany.

One day an old priest climbed the stairs in a quaint old building and knocked on that artist's door. He came to ask Stenburg if he would paint an altar piece for the church of Saint Jerome. The artist thought the matter over carefully before he answered. But he finally decided to do it. Little by little a picture of Christ dying for the sins of the world emerged on his canvas.

As the months rolled by, Stenburg began to experience a spirit of unrest. Spring had come creeping over the land and the green hills were covered with wild flowers. And so, the artist decided to lay his brushes aside for awhile. He took his sketchbook in hand and began roaming through the hills and valleys.

One day on the edge of the forest he came upon a young gypsy girl. She was sitting in the grass weaving daisy chains. Her beauty immediately captured his heart. He saw in her great potential. In a matter of minutes he convinced her that she should come to his studio where he could paint her as a little Spanish dancing girl.

The very first day she arrived in the studio, she noticed the emerging altarpiece. Her mind immediately was flooded with questions.

"Who is that?" she asked.

"The Christ," Stenburg responded rather nonchalantly.

"What are they doing to Him?" she continued.

"Crucifying Him." Stenburg replied with disinterest.

"But who are those people? Those people with all the ugly faces?" Her interest was growing and Stenburg was irritated. He told her to stop asking questions and to pose for him. And so she did.

However, the little girl's interest could not be stifled. So one day she ventured another question, since Stenburg seemed to be in a positive mood.

"Why did they do that to Him? Was He very bad?"

"No," the old artist responded sharply! "He was actually very good!"

Stenburg realized that he had to answer the little girl's questions once for all. And so, he laid down his brushes and told the story of Christ's crucifixion, warning her at the end of the story not to ask any more questions.

Finally the day arrived when Stenburg had completed his painting of the little gypsy girl. In that final moment before leaving, she took one long, hard look at the picture of Christ. She hardly noticed the coins Stenburg put in her hand for the final payment. As she turned to leave, she looked up into the artist's eyes and said, "You must love Him more than anything else in this world since He has done all that for you." And then she disappeared out the door and down the stairs.

Stenburg was startled! "Love Him?" he asked himself. "I don't love Him!"

The gypsy girl's final words became an obsession in Stenburg's mind. He couldn't forget them. Every morning when he walked into his studio and saw the picture of Christ, the words surfaced in his mind: "You must love Him more than anything else in this world since He has done all that for you."

Stenburg was actually very relieved when he finally completed the altarpiece and it was taken and placed in the church of Saint Jerome. He thought its absence would solve his problem. But it didn't! He found no rest in heart and soul.

Finally, after days of unrest, he discovered there were some special religious meetings that were being held in a home on the outskirts of Dusseldorf. "Perhaps I can find my answers there," he thought.

Mr. Stenburg made his way to a home where once again he

heard the story of the death of Christ. This time, however, it took on new meaning. He saw that Christ had died *for him*. He put his faith in Christ for salvation and became a Christian. It was then he was captured with a new desire. He wanted to do something for his Lord. He now truly loved Jesus Christ!

Stenburg thought long and hard about what he might do to express his love for His Saviour. And then one day, after asking God for direction, the thought flashed through his mind: "I cannot express the love of God by the use of words, but with His help I can paint it."

The face of Christ on the cross which he had painted for the church at Saint Jerome was full of agony and pain. But the picture of Christ he would now paint would be full of love.

Love burned in his own soul as he worked. The picture slowly emerged, showing the head and shoulders of Christ with a crown of thorns on His brow. It was a beautiful and inspiring picture. The eyes of Christ held the beholder spellbound. They were full of tender, eternal love.

When the picture was completed, Stenburg would not sell it. Rather, he gave it to the city of Dusseldorf and there it was hung in the art gallery. Under the painting he placed the words: "All this I did for thee; what has thou done for me?"

Thousands came and stood in front of the picture. As they looked, tears filled their eyes. Often Stenburg would go to the gallery and from some quiet corner watch the people who stood before it. As he watched he prayed that God would speak to them through the picture.

One day as he was watching, a young woman came into the gallery. She stationed herself before the picture and the artist could see that she was crying. She remained so long that at last he went to speak to her. And as she turned and faced him, Stenburg recognized the little gypsy girl—now a young woman—who had posed for him several years before. "I often come to look at Him," she explained apologetically. With quivering lips she said, "I wish He had loved me like that, but I'm only a gypsy."

Immediately Stenburg asked her forgiveness. He apologized for not having told the story accurately when she first asked her questions in the studio. With the girl's astonished eyes upon him, he told the story once again. But this time he explained the true meaning of the cross. And there in the art gallery, the gypsy girl gave her heart to the Saviour.

The years rolled by and each year added to the stories that were told of those who found God through Stenburg's painted sermon. One day a young nobleman entered the gallery and stood weeping before the picture. He was a Christian man, yet up to this time his life had not counted much for God. The painting with the words beneath sank into his heart. "All this I did for thee; what hast thou done for me?"

That day that young nobleman laid his life and his fortune at the feet of the Son of God. His name was Count Zinzendorf and later he became the founder of the Moravian missions.

Stenburg's painting is no longer in existence. It was burned when the Dusseldorf art gallery was destroyed by fire. But the story even to this day is not ended. The painting's influence will live on and on, forever, just as Paul's words will no doubt be repeated throughout eternity: "In him we have redemption though his blood, the forgiveness of sins" (Eph. 1:7).

With the hosts of heaven we'll sing: "Worthy is the Lamb, who was slain, to receive power and wealth and wisdom and strength and honor and glory and praise!" (Rev. 5:12).

4

Looking Up
To God The Spirit

And you also were included in Christ when you heard the word of truth, the gospel of your salvation. Having believed, you were marked in him with a seal, the promised Holy Spirit, who is a deposit guaranteeing our inheritance until the redemption of those who are God's possession—to the praise of his glory.

Over a quarter of a century ago, I picked up a lovely young lady in my freshly washed 1941 Chevrolet coupe. Elaine and I were spending the day together, heading for a recreational area in Central Illinois. A couple of months before, I had asked her to be my wife. She accepted.

As we headed south that day she had no idea that a special gift was carefully hidden away in a box of candy. I had carefully taken the cellophane from the box, removed a few chocolates from the center and replaced them with a ring box, wrapped in foil. When it was safely tucked away with the other "goodies," it looked like a huge chocolate mint. Inside the box was an engagement ring.

I then replaced the cellophane, sealed the edges with a hot iron, and placed the box in the glove compartment. It looked as though it had just come off the drugstore shelf.

While we were driving along I casually—but with my heart pounding—told Elaine I had bought some candy to munch on as we traveled. Totally unaware of what was about to happen, she finally got the wrapper off the box and opened it. I glanced at the open box, nearly dying inside, and said, "That one in the center looks large enough for both of us to eat. Why don't we share it first?" Unsuspectingly, Elaine took out what she thought was a gigantic piece of chocolate, removed the wrapping, and—you can imagine the look on her face. The ring was totally unexpected, since I had told her I was working toward getting it as a Christmas gift. But here it was a month early—on her birthday.

Neither of us will forget that moment together. When she placed the ring on her finger, our engagement was official!

The ring was in a sense a "downpayment" or "deposit" guaranteeing that Elaine was to become my wife and I her husband. It was no longer just a verbal agreement between us. Furthermore, it became a public fact. Everywhere we went, people would see we were engaged.

Paul tells us, in Ephesians 1:13-14, that when God sent His Spirit to indwell His people, He was a "deposit"—a downpayment—guaranteeing our inheritance until the redemption of those who are God's possession. In fact, the Greek word translated "deposit" in the *New International Version* was actually used, on occasion, to refer to a wedding ring. Let's look at this passage more clearly to see what Paul was actually saying.

THE SPIRIT'S ACTIONS

The Holy Spirit Opens Our Hearts to Understand the Gospel

To this point in the Ephesian letter Paul has outlined God's plan for us, and Christ's part in executing that plan. In this section he explains the Holy Spirit's part in personalizing these great realities in the heart of individual believers. Thus Paul wrote: "And you also were included in Christ when you heard the *word of truth,* the *gospel of your salvation*" (1:13).

What causes a person or a group of persons to respond to the "word of truth" as it is embodied in the message of Christ's death, burial and resurrection? These three realities are indeed the message of the gospel as Paul explained in his first letter to the Corinthians.

Paul's reference to the gospel: "Now, brothers, I want to remind you of the *gospel* I preached to you, which you received and on which you have taken your stand. By this *gospel* you are saved, if you hold firmly to the word I preached to you. Otherwise, you have believed in vain" (1 Cor. 15:1-2).

Paul's explanation of the gospel: "For what I received I passed on to you as of first importance: that *Christ died* for our sins according to the Scriptures, that *he was buried,* that *he was raised* on the third day according to the Scriptures" (15:3-4).

In view of this passage, let me repeat the question. What causes a person or a group of persons to respond to the gospel—the message that Christ died, was buried, and rose again? It is very clear that God uses human instruments to communicate the "word of truth" which Paul defined in Ephesians 1:13 as "the gospel" of our salvation. In this instance it was Paul and his fellow missionaries. Paul underscored the importance of human instrumentality in his Roman letter with a series of three questions:

• "How, then, can they call on the one they have not believed in?"

- "And how can they believe in the one of whom they have not heard?"
- "And how can they hear without someone *preaching to them*" (Rom. 10:14)?

God uses people to communicate His message. But there is only one Person who can open our hearts to *understand* the gospel. That Person is the Holy Spirit. Thus Paul wrote to the Corinthians that God has made known "a wisdom that has been hidden and that God destined for our glory before time began," and that "God has revealed it to us *by his Spirit*" (1 Cor. 2:7,10). Paul reminded these New Testament Christians that "none of the rulers of this age understood it, for if they had, they would not have crucified the Lord of glory" (2:8).

How then, can we come to know God's thoughts—these great truths Paul has outlined at the beginning of his Ephesian letter regarding the Father's plan and the work of His Son Jesus Christ in executing that plan? Paul answered this question specifically for the Corinthians: "We have not received the spirit of the world but the Spirit who is from God, that we may *understand* what God has freely given us" (2:12).

The Holy Spirit, then, opens our hearts to understand "the word of truth"—the gospel of our salvation.

The Holy Spirit Opens Our Hearts to Believe the Gospel

It is one thing to know and understand the gospel. It is yet another thing to believe it and receive the gift of salvation. Thus Paul wrote to the Ephesians: *"Having believed,* you were marked in him with a seal, the promised Holy Spirit" (1:13).

This truth is beautifully illustrated in Luke's record of the conversion of Lydia in Philippi. When Paul and his missionary team arrived in this Roman colony they found a group of women who had gathered for prayer on a river bank on the Sabbath day. Paul and his companions began to share the gospel. Luke, who was there and who also wrote the book of Acts, identified one of these ladies as Lydia. She was a businesswoman who manufactured and sold purple cloth. Though she worshiped God, she had never yet come to know Christ as her personal Saviour. We read that while Paul was sharing the gospel, *"the Lord opened her heart to respond* to Paul's message" (Acts 16:14).

This is a direct reference to the work of the Holy Spirit as He enables a person to respond and believe in the death, burial and resurrection of Jesus Christ. True, we respond with our own understanding and will, but the fact still remains that "no one can say, 'Jesus is Lord,' except by the Holy Spirit" (1 Cor. 12:3).

The Holy Spirit Places Us in the Body of Christ

When a person hears, understands and believes the gospel, something wonderful happens. We are "marked in him with a seal, the promised Holy Spirit." The Holy Spirit places us into the Body of Christ. We become a unique part of the family of God which the Bible calls the "Church." Again Paul makes this point clear in the Corinthian letter: "For we were *all baptized by one Spirit into one body*—whether Jews or Greeks, slave or free—and we were all given the one Spirit to drink" (12:13).

Every true believer has been baptized by the Holy Spirit. Though there are some who have had unusual experiences when this happened—especially in the early days of the Church—it is a transaction wrought by the Spirit of God that is true for every authentic Christian.

When I accepted Jesus Christ as my personal Saviour at age 16, I did not experience something unusual—except that I knew I was born again. I knew Christ had come to dwell in my heart. I knew my sins were forgiven. Though it took some time and lots of good teaching to understand what had happened, I knew I was God's child. After a long mental and psychological battle resisting the wooing of God's Holy Spirit, I had finally responded and turned by heart and life over to Him.

I remember it so well. It was on July 7, 1948. I was working out in the barnyard on our farm in Indiana. Two of my best friends—twin brothers—had become Christians and had shared with me their decision. I listened, but refused to accept Christ myself. "There are too many exciting things to do as a non-Christian," I thought.

I spent many days—and nights—in mental arguments with the Holy Spirit. But that day I remember throwing down the shovel I had in my hands and going into the house. I took one look at my mother and she knew why I had come to her side. She had witnessed my struggle with God. We went to my bed-room upstairs in the old farm home and knelt by my bed where I invited Jesus Christ into my life to be my personal Saviour. That day I was baptized into the Body of Christ by the Holy Spirit, who came to indwell my heart.

And so it is with every one who truly believes the gospel message. Psychological experiences may vary, but it is the same event. We are born again by the Spirit of God. It involves the same factors that Jesus explained to Nicodemus when he inquired about the new birth: "The wind blows wherever it pleases," Jesus answered. "You hear its sound, but you cannot tell where it comes from or where it is going. So it is with every-one born of the Spirit" (John 3:8).

THE BELIEVER'S BENEFITS

What does the presence of the Holy Spirit in a Christian's life actually mean? The answer to this question is Paul's next con-cern. The Holy Spirit "is a deposit guaranteeing our inheritance until the redemption of those who are God's possession" (Eph. 1:14).

When we truly believe in Christ we have eternal life (1:14; John 3:16). The presence of the Holy Spirit in our lives *guaran-tees our eternal salvation.* That is our inheritance. Some day we will receive new bodies. Jesus went to heaven to prepare a place for us (John 14:1-2).

Eternal life, of course, begins the moment we believe. But there will come a day when we will leave time and enter eter-nity. Then what we have hoped for and know to be true will be actually fulfilled. Death will be swallowed up in victory because the "perishable has been clothed with the imperishable, and the mortal with immortality" (1 Cor. 15:54). Our inheritance will be totally and completely ours. Our redemption will be completely realized.

Until then, Paul stated, we have a guarantee! It is a "deposit" or "downpayment," as it were. We have been "sealed" just as a package has been sealed for final delivery. Though life still goes on here, we know that our eternal life is secure in Jesus Christ because of God's Spirit who dwells in our lives.

Fortunately, God's seal will never be broken. His guarantee is absolute. "Nothing will be able to separate us from the love of God that is in Christ Jesus our Lord" (Rom. 8:39).

On the other hand, every human seal can be broken or nullified. Earlier I shared the experience of giving my wife Elaine an engagement ring. Later, we affirmed this downpayment with a wedding ring. And we are wearing our rings to this day.

In fact, Elaine gave me a brand new ring on our twenty-fifth anniversary. In a sense, she was getting even with me, for she never forgot the box of candy. For a long time she had anticipated our twenty-fifth anniversary weekend. Unknown to me, she was working with a jeweler, preparing a ring especially for me. I found out later she had the jeweler re-do it three times until it was just what she thought I'd like.

Then she planned a special weekend at a local hotel. To my surprise, when we arrived, she had brought along my racquetball equipment and informed me that she wanted me to teach her how to play the next day. Frankly, I was pleasantly surprised. She had never asked me before to teach her anything about sports.

The next day when we awakened, she handed me a brand new can of racquetballs that she had bought, and asked me to check them out. I opened the can and noticed that one of the balls was cracked and filled with white tissue paper. And when I pulled out the tissue paper, what do you suppose was there? Right! A lovely, twenty-fifth anniversary wedding ring. I was speechless. After 25 years she had out-capered my box of candy caper.

Today I'm thankful we're still married and more in love and committed to each other than the day we were married. True, we have been through the normal stresses and strains that accompany every marriage. Life has not always been a bowl of cherries or a rose garden—whatever metaphor you want to use. But we have remained true to our vows and have grown in our love for each other.

Marriage, of course, is a human illustration. There is no guarantee that couples will never separate, though God has designed marriage to be permanent. He is never pleased with divorce. In Christ, however, we have a much better chance of remaining true to our marriage vows because our commitments are more than human. They are divine.

In many respects what Paul is saying in this passage to the Ephesians is that as believers we are engaged to Christ, and that engagement will never be broken. And some day we will sit down at the "wedding supper of the Lamb" (Rev. 19:9). Eternal life will be culminated. Our redemption will be ultimately complete.

A PROPER RESPONSE

How should a Christian respond to the fact that we are secure in Christ? Again, Paul underscored this point as he did in verses 6 and 12. Since we are eternally to be "the praise of his glory," we should live lives worthy of this calling right now (Eph. 1:6,12,14). As Paul wrote to the Galatians, "Since we live by the Spirit, let us keep in step with the Spirit" (Gal. 5:25). This means we will reflect the fruit of the Spirit, which is "love, joy, peace, patience, kindness, goodness, faithfulness, gentleness and self-control" (5:22). If we "live by the Spirit," Paul wrote, we will not gratify the desires of this sinful nature—which are defined as "sexual immorality, impurity and debauchery; idolatry and witchcraft; hatred, discord, jealousy, fits of rage, selfish ambition, dissensions, factions and envy; drunkenness, orgies, and the like" (5:19-21).

A PERSONAL RESPONSE

An Affirmation

I BELIEVE IN GOD THE FATHER,
 Who raised Christ from the dead,
 Who created and sustains the universe,
 Who acts to deliver His people in times of need,
 Who desires all men everywhere to be saved.

I BELIEVE IN JESUS CHRIST HIS SON,

Who was promised to the people of Israel,
Who came in the flesh to dwell among us,
Who announced the coming of the rule of God,
Who gathered disciples and taught them,
Who rose from the dead to give us life and hope,
Who reigns in heaven at the right hand of God,
Who comes to judge and bring justice to victory.

I BELIEVE IN THE HOLY SPIRIT,

Who is the form of God present in the church,
Who is the guarantee of our deliverance,
Who leads us to find God's will in the Word,
Who guides us in discernment,
Who impels us to act together.

5

Learning To Know God Better

EPHESIANS 1:15-17

For this reason, ever since I heard about your faith in the Lord Jesus and your love for all the saints, I have not stopped giving thanks for you, remembering you in my prayers. I keep asking that the God of our Lord Jesus Christ, the glorious Father, may give you the Spirit of wisdom and revelation, so that you may know him better.

Charles Colson, at the conclusion of his third book, *Loving God,* penned these encouraging words:

> It is exactly ten years since I visited my dear friend, Tom Phillips, as the Watergate scandal exploded across the nation's press. Though I felt an awful deadness inside, I didn't think I was searching spiritually. But while Tom's explanation that he had "accepted Jesus Christ" shocked and baffled me, it also made me curious. He was at peace with himself, something I surely wasn't.
>
> Tom explained it all to me that sultry August night. I couldn't show too much interest, of course—I was senior partner of a powerful law firm, friend of the President. But as I left Tom's house, I discovered I couldn't get my keys into the car ignition. I couldn't see them. The White House "hatchet man" as the newspapers called me, the ex-Marine infantry captain was crying too hard. That night I was confronted with my own sin—not just Watergate's dirty tricks, but the sin deep within me, the hidden evil that lives in every human heart. It was painful and I could not escape. I cried out to God and found myself driven irresistibly into His waiting arms. That was the night I gave my life to Jesus Christ and began the greatest adventure of my life.
>
> A lot of skeptics thought it wouldn't last, that it was just a ploy for sympathy, a foxhole conversion. I don't blame them. If the tables were turned I'd have thought the same thing.
>
> But not once in these ten years have I doubted that Jesus Christ lives. There is nothing of which I am more certain. And not once would I have turned the clock back. My lowest days as a Christian (and there were low ones—seven months worth of them in prison, to be exact) have been more fulfilling and

rewarding than all the days of glory in the White
House. The years before conversion were death.
The years since have been life and the adventure of
loving God, the purpose of that life.

And so with each passing day, my gratitude to God
for what He did for me—at Calvary and that night in
my friend's driveway—grows deeper and deeper.[1]

Chuck Colson's conversion to Christ and his steady growth
in his Christian life is a real encouragement to me personally. I
began to read his first book, *Born Again,* somewhat out of curiosity. As I read I was encouraged by the fact that Jesus Christ is
still in the business of saving people who have built their lives
around their own selfish ambitions.

When I read Chuck's second book, *Life Sentence,* I was even
more encouraged. Here was a man who came to know Jesus
Christ as his personal Saviour, but was remarkably changed.
And as I've been reading his third book, I'm captivated by Mr.
Colson's desire to know God better.

A PRAYER OF THANKSGIVING

Paul's concern for the Ephesian Christians and others who
had come to know Christ in other parts of Asia was that they
know God better. Converted to Christ out of a pagan life-style,
which was characterized by total selfishness and sin, they began
the process of spiritual growth. Paul commended them for their
"faith in the Lord Jesus and [their] *love* for all the saints" (Eph.
1:15). Because of their spiritual growth, both as individuals and
as a church body, his heart was overflowing with thanksgiving to
God—so much so, he wrote: "I have not stopped giving thanks
for you, remembering you in my prayers" (1:16).

One of the greatest rewards for any Christian is to see someone he has won to Christ grow spiritually. Think how Tom Phil-
lips must have felt when he first read Chuck Colson's book, *Loving God.* "Could it be," he must have asked himself, "that this is
the ruthless politician who came to visit me 10 years ago?"

As I stand before the people in my own church each week, the greatest thrill is to see people who have found Christ and are growing spiritually. I think of Greg who, two years ago, accepted Christ in my office, and just this week (as I'm writing this) worked together with me on a very significant spiritual project. I think of Jackie who sat in church for a couple of years as a skeptic but who finally gave her life to Jesus Christ and has grown in a wonderful way over the last several years.

Conversely, I look out over the audience each week and notice that some people are missing—people who used to respond to the Word of God with positive nods and eager smiles. Some, of course, are attending other churches and are growing spiritually. I rejoice when that is true, for it matters not where a person worships as long as he or she is being fed the Word of God and is growing spiritually.

But I also see those in my mind's eye who are no longer worshiping with God's people anywhere. They are living once again in their own self-centered world. Some are disillusioned with Christianity. Some have been inundated with the cares of this life and their priorities are not in order. Some are angry for one reason or another. Some are living in serious sin. Others are just nominal Christians with little interest in spiritual growth.

Frankly, this is the most painful part of the ministry. Conversely, Christians who respond and continue to strive to know God better make it all worthwhile. And thus Paul wrote: "For this reason, ever since I heard about your faith in the Lord Jesus and your love for all the saints, I have not stopped giving thanks for you, remembering you in my prayers."

A PETITION FOR GROWTH

Paul was never satisfied with his own spiritual status or that of other Christians. He knew that in many respects his own Christian life was always in process of *becoming*—becoming more and more like Jesus. Of himself he wrote: "Not that I have already obtained all this, or have already been made perfect, but I press on to take hold of that for which Christ Jesus took hold of me. Brothers, I do not consider myself yet to have taken hold of it. But one thing I do: Forgetting what is behind and straining toward what is ahead, I press on toward the goal to win the prize for which God has called me heavenward in Christ Jesus" (Phil. 3:12-14).

Consequently, when he wrote to the Ephesians, though he was delighted with their faith and love, he went on to say, "I keep asking that the God of our Lord Jesus Christ, the glorious Father, may give you the Spirit of wisdom and revelation, *so that you may know him better*" (Eph. 1:17).

What did Paul have in mind when he prayed that God might give these Ephesian Christians "the Spirit of wisdom and revelation"? To answer this question, it might help to establish first of all what Paul *didn't* mean.

What Paul Was NOT Teaching

He was not praying that they might receive the Holy Spirit.

These Christians had already received the Spirit. A few verses earlier Paul had reminded them that since they had received Christ and believed in Him, they had been "marked in him with a seal, the promised Holy Spirit" (Eph. 1:13). In Romans Paul stated that "if anyone does not have the Spirit of Christ, he does not belong to Christ" (Rom. 8:9).

He was not referring to some kind of special anointing by the Spirit.

Throughout Christian history there are Christians who have looked for some kind of special experience with the Holy Spirit. When this so-called experience comes, they believe they have reached a new level of spirituality. Some call this "the baptism of the Spirit"—a special work of grace after salvation. However, the Bible teaches that *all Christians* are baptized by the Spirit the moment they become Christians (1 Cor. 12:13).

This is not to deny that the Holy Spirit can do special things in a Christian's life any time He wants to. In fact, many of the Christians God has used in great ways have testified to a special anointing. I am reminded of D. L. Moody who testified to this very thing. Following a unique experience with the Holy Spirit he felt that God's blessing was upon his evangelistic ministry in unusual ways. Something was different.

However, the Scriptures do not teach that this is a "normative" experience for every believer and something we should seek. No doubt God does choose some Christians for special tasks—even today. The danger is, of course, that we search after this kind of experience and become disillusioned when something special doesn't happen. In fact, some Christians conclude that God can't use them because they have not had the same experience as someone else. In this sense, it is dangerous to compare experiences. For one thing, it's easy to conjure up an emotional experience, confuse it with a spiritual experience and, in the process, deceive ourselves and others.

He was not referring to some kind of special gifts of the Spirit.

There are some, of course, who will want to debate this issue. The goal of Paul's prayer is that these believers might "know [God] better." However, nowhere in Scripture are spiritual gifts related to spiritual maturity per se.

The Corinthians illustrate this graphically. They had more gifts of the Spirit than any other New Testament church, and yet Paul rebuked them more in his letters than he did any other church. In fact, their gifts were actually interfering with their spiritual growth—creating spiritual pride, divisions and continued immaturity.

Paul made this point clear in 1 Corinthians 13. Appealing to them to follow the way of love, he wrote: "Love never fails.
- But where there are prophecies [a gift of the Spirit], they will cease;
- where there are tongues [a gift of the Spirit], they will be stilled;
- where there is knowledge (a gift of the Spirit), it will pass away.

For we know in part and we prophesy in part, but when perfection [that is, maturity] comes, the imperfect [that is, immaturity] disappears" (1 Cor. 13:8-10).

Paul then used an illustration to contrast immaturity and

maturity. He wrote: "When I was a *child,* I talked like a *child,* I thought like a *child,* I reasoned like a *child.* When I became a *man,* I put *childish ways* behind me" (13:11).

This leads us back to the question, What did Paul mean when he informed the Ephesian Christians that he kept on asking God to give them "the Spirit of wisdom and revelation"? Before we can answer that question we need to look at the reason for this prayer: "So that you may *know him better*" (Eph. 1:17).

The key word in Paul's statement, both in the Corinthian letter and the Ephesian letter, is the word "know." There is a normal word for "know" in the Greek text—the word *gnosis.* But there's another word for "know" in the New Testament. When a preposition is added to the word *gnosis,* you have the word *epi-gnosis.* This is the word Paul used in his prayer for the Ephesians. It means a "deep and full knowledge of God." The normal word *gnosis* simply means "first awareness" or an "initial and superficial acquaintance with some one or thing."

Paul illustrates the distinction between these two words in the Corinthian passage we just looked at. He wrote: "Now I *know in part* [that is, initial knowledge]; then I shall *know fully*" [that is, have complete and full knowledge—*epi-gnosis*)] (1 Cor. 13:12).

In this passage Paul contrasted the knowledge of God on this earth with the knowledge of God in heaven. This is certainly a legitimate contrast. But the Corinthian knowledge of God when Paul wrote this letter was very superficial, in spite of their giftedness. But Paul's letter to the Ephesians and his prayer for them makes it very clear that we do not need to wait until we're in heaven to begin to experience a deep and full knowledge of God.

To understand even more clearly what Paul was praying for, compare his parallel prayer for the Colossian Christians: "For this reason, since the day we heard about you, we have not stopped praying for you and asking God to *fill you with the knowledge of his will through all spiritual wisdom and understanding.* And we pray this in order that you may live a life worthy of the Lord and may please him in every way: bearing fruit in every good work, *growing in the knowledge of God*" (Col. 1:9-10).

Compare also his prayer for the Philippians: "And this is my prayer: that your love may abound more and more in *knowledge* and *depth of insight,* so that you may be able to *discern* what is best and may be pure and blameless until the day of Christ, filled with the fruit of righteousness that comes through Jesus Christ—to the glory and praise of God" (Phil. 1:9-11).

What Paul WAS Teaching

From these parallel passages it is clear what Paul was praying for the Ephesians: He wanted them to know God better by knowing more about Him, both intellectually and experientially. The primary means was God's revelation of Himself through Jesus Christ, the living Word of God; the Scriptures; the written Word of God; and the indwelling Holy Spirit who illumines our minds and hearts to understand the will of God through the Word of God.

PERSONALIZING PAUL'S PRAYER

How can you and I get to know God better?

Through the Word of God

Our primary source for getting to know God better is His Word. As we study the Bible, a profile of God emerges, of what He is really like. There we see His attributes: that He is holy; that He is all-powerful; that He is all-knowing; that He has the ability to be present everywhere; that He is eternal; and, perhaps most of all, that He is immanent and personal. He really cares about me and you! He is a loving heavenly Father.

If I am to come to know God better, then it is important that I read and study the Bible on a regular basis, allowing the Holy Spirit who dwells within me to enlighten my heart and mind.

Through His Natural Creation

Paul wrote to the Romans, "For since the creation of the world God's invisible qualities—his eternal power and divine nature—have been clearly seen, being understood from what has been made, so that men are without excuse (Rom. 1:20).

I enjoy snow skiing. There are several reasons. First, it's just plain fun. Also, it's a great form of exercise—and God knows I need as much of that as I can get. And for me, it is one of those activities where I can forget everything that is occupying my mind—all of the people problems that a pastor faces every day. When you ski you have to concentrate totally on what you're doing. If you don't, it's bottoms up—you'll find yourself facedown in a mound of snow.

But, the most exciting part of skiing for me is to stand at the top of a gigantic snow-covered mountain on a beautiful sunshiny day, looking out beyond to dozens of other snow-covered peaks. There they stand, jagged and dazzling white against a glorious blue sky. During those awesome moments, I've often exclaimed to those skiing with me, "Just think, the majority of people in the world will never see this view of God's marvelous handiwork!"

I get chills just thinking about those sights. God made all that, and yet He cares about me! That's true. He didn't send His Son to redeem the universe or to save mountains, even snow-covered ones. He sent His Son to redeem me, to make it possible for me to know Him through His Son Jesus Christ. Yes, God's creation is one way in which we can come to know God better.

Through Others Who Know Him Well

This is perhaps the most powerful means of all. Jesus said to His disciples, "All men will know that you are my disciples if you love one another" (John 13:35).

The Apostle John, who heard these words as he reclined at the table that night with Jesus, later came to know much more fully what Jesus actually had in mind. In his first Epistle he wrote: "Dear friends, since God so loved us, we also ought to love one another. No one has ever seen God; but if we love each other, God lives in us and his love is made complete in us" (1 John 4:11-12).

Here John was saying that God cannot be seen since He is Spirit. Also at this point in time, Jesus Christ, who revealed God's love and character, had returned to heaven. How then can we know what God is like? John answers that question: When

God's "love is made complete in us."

This has profound implications for helping others to come to know God better. We all need models of godliness. Perhaps the most profound implication is in the home and falls squarely on the shoulders of those of us who are fathers.

I've often shared the story of overhearing my two daughters when they were very small having a little-girl conversation one day. One said to the other with a stroke of insight, "You know, God is our heavenly Daddy!"

They did not know I was listening, but my heart was impacted beyond measure. It dawned on me for the first time that how they viewed God was how they viewed me. I was in their eyes a representative of the heavenly Father.

Thank God that He does not lay this burden to represent Him on fathers and mothers exclusively. We all fail. Thus, He has designed the Church—the Body of Christ—which should be filled with multiple models of godliness. First, there are the leaders of the church—those of us who are to measure up to the qualities outlined by Paul so clearly in his Epistles (1 Tim. 3; Titus 1). But also, there is every member of the Body of Christ. Fortunately, God has designed a plan to overcome our failures as parents. There are other models of godliness who can balance out our weaknesses, thus giving our children a more well-rounded view of who God really is and what He is really like. Our goal then, as individual Christians and as a Body of believers, should be to represent God as He really is to all other Christians—and to non-Christians!

A PROCESS INVOLVING EFFORT

Coming to know God better is not automatic. Even prayer is not the final means. Though Paul prayed that the Ephesian Christians might come to know God better, it wouldn't just happen. It involved effort on their part.

Let me illustrate. I remember sitting in a classroom when I was attending the Wheaton Graduate School. Dr. Merrill Tenney, a professor who impacted my life greatly, was teaching the Gospel of John. The text he was expounding was John 17:3, which reads: "Now this is eternal life: that they may *know* you, the only true God, and Jesus Christ, whom you have sent."

Dr. Tenney pointed out that some believe that Jesus is referring to the fact that we will spend all eternity coming to know God. To make this point clear, he used a human illustration. It involved marriage. "When you court the person you're going to marry," he shared, "you are coming to know that person. Granted, your exposure is superficial. The relationship is just beginning."

And then, Dr. Tenney pointed out, you eventually get married. Then the process of coming to know that person *really* begins. My professor then mentioned that at that point in time he had been married for many years. "Yet," he said, "I am still coming to know my wife and she is still coming to know me. And one of the reasons," he said, "is that we're both made in the image of God." There is tremendous depth to the human personality.

That illustration impacted my own life, especially since at that time I was single. But I never forgot it. And how true I have found that illustration to be. As I look back over a quarter of a century of marriage, I realize that my knowledge of Elaine just began when we were married. In fact, I must confess that my knowledge of her was quite superficial for quite a few years, even after we were married. And then one day we began to share more deeply our inner thoughts and feelings. It resulted from a crisis, precipitated by the fact that I was so involved with other people and projects that I, in reality, was neglecting her. For the first time in my life I sat and listened to her pour out her feelings of frustration about our relationship.

Though it was painful for me to listen, for the first time in our marriage I really began to know Elaine. I saw how committed she had been to me though for years I tended to put my studies and my work in first place. I understood her hurts that day. I sensed and identified with her frustration.

I was teaching full-time at Dallas Theological Seminary and I had a heavy schedule planned for the day. However, I made a decision at that moment that was one of the best I've made in my life. I called the seminary and cancelled my classes for the day and just spent time with my wife, listening. Since that time I've come to know my wife even better. I know there are many things I still need to learn. I am still tempted to become so involved in other things that I neglect her. But things are different now. Even so, I still have to work at it *every day*.

And just so, if we are to come to know God better we must work at getting to know Him. We must pay attention when He speaks. We must sit quietly in His presence and listen to His voice. We must give Him the best of our time, not what is left over.

This, in essence, is what Paul was praying for the Ephesians. They had made a great beginning. They had a strong faith in the Lord Jesus. They also exemplified deep love for their fellow Christians. This was cause for rejoicing. But Paul said, "I keep asking that the God of our Lord Jesus Christ, the glorious Father, may give you the Spirit of wisdom and revelation, so that you may *know him better.*"

Note

1. Taken from LOVING GOD, by Charles Colson. Copyright © 1983 by Charles W. Colson. Used by permission of Zondervan Publishing House.

6

Understanding Our Hope

EPHESIANS 1:18-19

I pray also that the eyes of your heart may be enlightened in order that you may know the hope to which he has called you, the riches of his glorious inheritance in the saints, and his incomparably great power for us who believe.

Have you ever been on a roller coaster? Imagine for a moment you never really knew where it all would end when you climbed aboard and buckled in. It might level out and end its wild journey safely at another point. Or, at some point along the way, it might leave the track and speed off into space—and crash and burn!

There are some Christians who live their lives as if they are on a spiritual and emotional roller coaster. They're really not sure where they are going to end up in eternity—safely in heaven or eternally separated from God because of some mistake they might have made along the way.

The believers Paul was writing to in the Ephesian letter had difficulty accepting the fact that their salvation was secure in Christ. The reason for this will become increasingly clear as we study further in this Epistle. But in this chapter let's look at what Paul said to encourage them.

The fact that Paul was concerned about their sense of security in Christ is focused in the middle of his prayer for these New Testament believers. He had already prayed that they may *come to know God better* (Eph. 1:17). He then prayed: "I pray also that the eyes of your heart may be enlightened in order that you may know the *hope to which he has called you,* the riches of his glorious inheritance in the saints, and his incomparably great power for us who believe" (1:18-19).

"THE HOPE TO WHICH HE HAS CALLED YOU"

What does the Bible mean by the word "hope"?

The concept of the word "hope" has two dimensions: first, the meaning of the word itself; and, second, what this kind of hope produces in our lives. The word "hope" indicates that we have assurance of eternal life. Note the following references that make this point clear:

- "But since we belong to the day, let us be self-controlled, putting on faith and love as a breastplate, and *the hope of salvation* as a helmet" (1 Thess. 5:8).
- "A faith and knowledge resting on the *hope of eternal life,*

which God, who does not lie, promised before the beginning of time" (Titus 1:2).

- "We wait for the *blessed hope*—the glorious appearing of our great God and Savior, Jesus Christ, who gave himself for us to redeem us" (2:13-14).
- "In his great mercy he has given us new birth into a *living hope* through the resurrection of Jesus Christ from the dead, and into an inheritance that can never perish, spoil or fade—kept in heaven for you" (1 Pet. 1:3-4).

When a Christian truly understands the hope he has in Christ, it results in a steadfast sense of security and stability. Note the following references which illustrate these results.

- "We continually remember before our God and Father . . . your *endurance inspired by hope* in our Lord Jesus Christ (1 Thess. 1:3).
- "Let us hold *unswervingly to the hope* we profess, for he who promised is faithful" (Heb. 10:23).
- "Command those who are rich in this present world not to be arrogant nor to put their *hope in wealth,* which is so *uncertain,* but to put their *hope in God,* who richly provides us with everything for our enjoyment" (1 Tim. 6:17).
- "*Set your hope* fully on the grace to be given you when Jesus Christ is revealed" (1 Pet. 1:13).

Is it possible to be relatively strong in faith and love and yet weak in hope?

Paul had already thanked God for the *faith* these Christians had in Christ, and their *love* for one anther (Eph. 1:15). However, in this part of his prayer, he asked that they might know the *hope* to which God had called them. This indicates there was some uncertainty in their lives regarding their eternal destiny.

"How can this be?" you might ask. Is it possible to have faith in Christ and manifest the love of Christ, and yet not be secure and have a sense of steadfastness in Christ? Christians who have been taught that their salvation is secure in Christ have difficulty identifying with these Ephesian believers. But those of us who have been reared in an environment where salvation is related to works can easily identify with the Ephesians. I certainly can!

I was reared in a religious community that had its roots in

Switzerland and was started by Samuel Froehlich. Though reared in a Christian home, he became a rationalist while studying at the University of Basel. However, through the study of Scripture he eventually put his faith in Jesus Christ. From the historical record there is no question but that this man truly became a Christian in October of 1825.

In 1827 Froehlich was ordained to the ministry in the protestant state church. However, when he discovered that this church was influenced by the same rationalism that had led him astray, he took a stand against what he felt were abuses in the church. Consequently, he was excommunicated and eventually started a new group. As members of this group migrated to America, they eventually formed a denomination called the Apostolic Christian Church.

Though Froehlich became a true believer and eventually reacted to the rationalism in the protestant state church, the theology he developed included "works" in his formula for salvation. Over the years the system became even more and more works-oriented.

I was greatly influenced by this theology that mixed faith and works for salvation. I often felt as if I were on a spiritual and emotional roller-coaster, never certain that my final descent would ever level out and come to a safe stop. If I felt good emotionally, I then believed that everything was alright between myself and God. If I felt emotionally down, I became very uncertain of my standing before God. If I failed God in some way— lost my temper, was tempted with some evil thoughts, became too frivolous, wasn't concerned about others as I should be, didn't feel like praying or reading the Bible (all normal feelings and thoughts)—then I seriously questioned my eternal relationship with God. Obviously, my spiritual life was chaotic.

Little by little, through personal study of the Bible, attending youth conferences outside my religious community and, through listening to a Christian radio station, I developed a desire to attend a Christian school to learn more about the Scriptures. And so I did, enrolling at Moody Bible Institute in Chicago, which eventually led to my excommunication from this religious group.

Outside of accepting Jesus Christ as my personal Saviour, this decision turned out to be the most significant one of my life. It was at Moody Bible Institute that I discovered that my salvation was secure in Christ—that I had *hope*—and that I could know for sure, every moment of every day, that my eternal inheritance was guaranteed.

That assurance did not come about without a desperate struggle. For years I had been taught that I could not know for sure that I had eternal life until I awakened in eternity and heard God's final words of acceptance or rejection. Even when the truth of Scripture came ringing through loud and clear, the traditions I had been taught often blocked out the reality of these great scriptural statements and filled my heart with doubts. But eventually the "eyes of my heart" were enlightened by the Holy Spirit and I began to understand the hope to which God has called me.

Don't misunderstand. I was a Christian even though I did not accept my eternal position in Christ. I believed in God and His Son Jesus Christ. I had faith that Jesus died for me. And I loved my brothers and sisters in Christ. In fact, the church I grew up in was a very caring community—particularly among themselves. However, I constantly wavered in my hope. It depended upon the circumstances of the moment.

I share this story to illustrate that it *is* possible to have faith in Christ and love for others—but to have little hope, even as a true believer. This is still true among many believers today and it was no doubt true of a large segment of the Ephesian Christians. Thus Paul prayed that they might "know the hope" to which God had called them (1:18).

"THE RICHES OF HIS GLORIOUS INHERITANCE IN THE SAINTS"

Paul had two primary concerns for the Ephesian Christians when he wrote his letter. He wanted them, *first*, to truly know and understand the *hope* to which God had called them; *second*, he wanted them to live a life worthy of that calling (Eph. 4:1). Paul focused this first concern in his prayer.

In retrospect, we can now understand more fully why he began his letter with the great doctrinal realities that explain our "spiritual blessings in Christ" (1:3). His opening section, (particularly verses 3-14) is foundational to his major concern. This in turn helps us to understand what Paul meant when he prayed that the Christians might know "the riches of his glorious inheritance in the saints" (1:18).

Paul used the word *riches* six times in the first three chapters of this letter to describe a believer's blessings in Christ (1:18; 2:4,7; 3:8,16).

How rich is a Christian? Paul has already carefully outlined these riches in verses 3-14. Let's review:

God the Father has:
- Chosen us in Christ before the foundation of the world (1:4)
- Predestined us to be adopted as His sons (1:5).

God the Son has:
- Executed God's plan by shedding His blood on the cross (1:7)
- Redeemed us through His blood and provided forgiveness of sins (1:7).

God the Spirit has:
- Enabled us to respond in faith to God's love (1:13)
- Guaranteed our inheritance (1:14).

What Paul outlined in the first part of this letter is indeed the basis of a Christian's hope. Furthermore, it helps us to understand "the riches of his glorious inheritance in the saints." Thus we see that this part of Paul's prayer for the Ephesians is intricately related to knowing and understanding the hope to which He has called us. If these believers really understood the riches of their glorious inheritance, they would indeed have hope. They would not waver and be unstable in their Christian lives.

"HIS INCOMPARABLY GREAT POWER FOR US WHO BELIEVE"

A Christian's hope and inheritance is not based on human effort. If it were, we'd surely lose it all! Rather, our position in Christ is based on God's omnipotence—"his incomparably great power." This aspect of our salvation and hope is so significant that Paul elaborated on it at length—which is the basis of our next chapter.

Needless to say, there is no power greater than God's power. We can trust that power not only to provide us with our inheritance in Christ but to guarantee that no other force in the universe can take it away from us. This is why Paul wrote to the Romans: "For I am convinced that neither death nor life, neither angels nor demons, neither the present nor the future, nor any *powers*, neither height nor depth, nor anything else in all creation, will be able to separate us from the love of God that is in Christ Jesus our Lord" (Rom. 8:38,39).

WHAT DOES HAVING "HOPE" MEAN IN THE DAILY ROUTINES OF LIFE?

First, it means we can rest in God's love and grace. We can be sure of our salvation. Our emotional ups and downs and spiritual failures do not affect our inheritance.

To be sure, this does not give us a license to sin. As we'll see later, these great truths, rightly understood, will draw us closer to God and motivate us to "live lives worthy of God, who calls [us] into his kingdom and glory" (1 Thess. 2:12).

Second, having hope in Christ means we have something to share with others who do not have eternal hope. The great majority of people on planet earth have fixed their hope on things that will eventually fade and pass away. And when that happens, they have no hope whatsoever. There is *nothing* to cling to.

Years ago, off the coast of Massachusetts, an S-4 submarine was rammed by another ship and before anyone could escape from the wounded vessel, it sank. The entire crew was trapped in its prison house of death.

A number of ships immediately rushed to the scene of the disaster. But there was nothing they could do. They could only watch and wait. However, they did send down divers to evaluate the tragic situation.

One of the men put his helmeted ear against the side of the vessel and listened. Faintly, but clearly, he heard a tapping noise. Trained in Morse code, he recognized the "dots and dashes" and immediately deciphered the message: "Is—there—any—hope?"

Hopefully, someone outside that trapped submarine knew the answer to that desperate question—which at that critical moment became an eternal question. When all else fails, there is an answer. And people, no matter what their status in life, are asking that question.

My brother Wally, who serves on our pastoral staff, was visiting a young man in the hospital who had cancer. Through a series of circumstances he had met this man while visiting another cancer patient. As he walked into his room that day, the patient, who had already lost his hearing from this dreaded disease, spoke softly and yet with a sense of finality.

"Wally, I'm not going to make it," he said. He immediately began to give instructions to his wife about what he wanted for his funeral. Then he turned to Wally and continued: "Would you say a few words? I don't want a lot of things said; I just want you to be there and say a few words at the funeral."

Wally, knowing Dick could not hear him, took a sheet of paper and wrote these words:

> Dick, thank you for asking me to say a few words.
> The most important words that I could say are that I
> am sure that you are in heaven with Jesus. You can
> be sure by asking Jesus into your life. The Bible
> teaches that this is truth; and the truth will make you
> free.

As Dick read the note, he nodded positively, as if to say, "Yes, this is what I want; this is what I need."

As Wally left the room, the man's wife followed him, explaining with a tearful voice that her husband did not know what he was saying when he was talking about death.

"Oh, yes he does," Wally responded, calling her by name. You see, my brother had gone through the painful experience of seeing his own wife die from cancer. With compassion and yet directness, he told this young woman that she must come to grips with what her husband was sharing. "He's dying!" Wally stated. "And barring a miracle he won't live."

At that moment, the young woman seemed to come to grips with the reality of death. From a human point of view there was no hope. But in Christ there was hope, hope beyond the grave and a hope that even cancer could not take away.

This, then, is one of the most practical applications of what Paul was praying for the Ephesians and for us. We can offer hope to hurting people. Death is no respecter of persons. All the money in the world at this moment does not offer hope. All of our status, position, talents, abilities will not provide hope. True, there is power in positive thinking. Many problems in our physical bodies *are* created because we think negatively. Furthermore, if God so chooses, He can heal a dying person. But there is a point at which we must all face eternity. All the positive thinking in the world will not change this reality. We are born to die unless Jesus Christ comes before we each face that moment.

WHAT ABOUT YOU?

Are you sure of your eternal destiny? You can be, by accepting Jesus Christ as your personal Saviour.

If you have accepted Jesus Christ as your personal Saviour, do you have moment-by-moment security in Christ?

If you do not, you can, for Jesus said He would never leave nor forsake you.

Are you sharing this hope with others? You should be, for people everywhere are desperately crying out for hope. Sometimes the signal is very weak or in a different form—just as the dot-dot-dash-dash signal that was coming from that trapped submarine. Sometimes it is camouflaged by anger and defensiveness. Sometimes it is hidden behind a wall of silence. Sometimes it is buried deep within and is even covered by a ready smile. But when we understand the signal that people are sending out we can answer back with assurance. "Yes—there—is—hope—in—Jesus—Christ!"

7

Understanding God's Power

EPHESIANS 1:19-23

That power is like the working of his mighty strength, which he exerted in Christ when he raised him from the dead and seated him at his right hand in the heavenly realms, far above all rule and authority, power and dominion, and every title that can be given, not only in the present age but also in the one to come. And God placed all things under his feet and appointed him to be head over everything for the church, which is his body, the fullness of him who fills everything in every way.

On May 18, 1980, in the state of Washington, there was an incredible explosion, estimated at 500 times the force of the atomic bomb that destroyed Hiroshima. So great was the blast that it ripped 1,200 feet off the top of a 9,700-foot volcano named Mount St. Helens.

Geologists say that the peak exploded following the buildup of pressure from gas and magma (molten rock) inside the mountain, which had been dormant for 123 years. The blast emitted thousands of tons of volcanic ash into the atmosphere. In less than seven days, a cloud of volcanic gas containing some toxic chemicals and minute particles of radioactive substances spread over most of North America.

Within minutes after the explosion a cloud of ash blocked out the sun in the immediate area and turned day into night in surrounding communities. Friends of mine who live approximately 150 miles east of the volcano reported that they heard the explosion and shortly thereafter saw the great billowy cloud headed in their direction. Within a couple of hours, about noonday, the sun was blotted out, and day turned as dark as midnight. A powdery ash began to fall like a winter snowstorm, dumping from four to six inches of powdery substance that virtually immobilized their community.

The immediate area surrounding Mount St. Helens was a prime hunting and fishing country, a popular area for hiking and horseback riding, a productive place for rock hounds, a paradise for campers. *Sports Illustrated* reported however that "the eruption changed all that in an instant. Heat, blast and ash destroyed 26 lakes, 154 miles of resident trout streams and 195 square miles of wildlife habitat."

This demonstration of power is no doubt one of the most dramatic of its kind in this century for those of us who live in the United States. But, may I remind you that in the year 1883, Mount Krakatoa, in Indonesia, erupted, releasing energy estimated by scientists that was equal to 30 hydrogen bombs. If the energy released from Mount St. Helens was equal to the power of 500 atomic bombs, then the power released from Mount Krakatoa was equal to 30,000 atomic bombs (the explosive force of one hydrogen bomb is 1,000 times more powerful than one atomic bomb). During that great natural catastrophe, tidal waves killed 36,000 people in Java and Sumatra, and the cloud of ash cooled the earth's climate for nearly two years.

Since dynamite was first produced in 1867 by Alfred Nobel, a Swedish chemist, we have come a long way in understanding firsthand the incredible power that can be generated on planet Earth. Whether harnessed and then released by man, or suddenly unleashed through volcanic eruption, earthquakes, or floods, we understand more clearly than ever the incredible energy that can be generated through explosions and uncontrolled natural elements. But whether contrived by man or spontaneously released by nature, the fact is that they all reflect God's power.

The incredible energy generated by Mount St. Helens and Mount Krakatoa provides a graphic backdrop for better understanding Paul's prayer for the Ephesian Christians. Thus far we have seen that he prayed that God might give them "the spirit of wisdom and revelation" so that they might *know Him better!* (Eph. 1:17). Next he prayed "that the eyes of [their] heart may be enlightened in order that they may know the *hope* to which he has called" them (1:18). In this study we will see a third request in his prayer: that they may know God's "incomparably great *power* for us who believe."

GOD'S POWER DESCRIBED

Paul wanted to make sure the Ephesians clearly understood the *concept* of God's power. Consequently, he used four Greek words, all basically synonymous terms, to describe this power: "I pray also that the eyes of your heart may be enlightened in order that you may know . . . his incomparably great *power* for us who believe. That *power* is like the *working* of his *mighty strength*" (Eph. 1:18-19).

The word "power" comes from the basic Greek word *dunamis*, from which we get our word "dynamite." The term "working" comes from the basic Greek word *energeia* from which we get our English word "energy." The word "mighty" comes from the basic Greek word *kratos* and the word "strength" comes from the basic Greek word *ischus*.

Though all of these words indicate "power," one commentator sees different shades of meaning:

- Power—the ability to accomplish what is planned, promised or started.
- Working—inherent strength or brute power.
- Mighty—power to resist and overcome obstacles or opponents.
- Strength—the actual exercise of power.

Thus Markus Barth translates "What is the exceeding greatness of His *power* . . . in accordance with the *energy* of the *force* of His *strength*."[1]

These four words graphically describe God's omnipotence. He definitely has the ability to carry out what He has planned and promised. Inherent in His very nature is strength and power. There is no obstacle or force that can withstand His might.

Note also that Paul prefaces this string of synonyms by identifying the "working" of God's "mighty strength" as "his *incomparably great* power." Literally, Paul was saying there is no power greater than the power he was defining, including the power released at Mount St. Helens and by Krakatoa in Indonesia.

GOD'S POWER DEMONSTRATED

Paul went on to describe God's power as that "which he exerted in Christ when he raised him from the dead and seated him at his right hand in the heavenly realms" (1:20).

Paul's major concern was that these Christians understand fully the power that was demonstrated in Christ, first when He was raised from the dead; and second, when He once again ascended to be with the Father. This act of God was so remarkable that Paul described it in detail.

First he said that this power placed Christ "far above all rule and authority, power and dominion, and every title that can be given, not only in the present age, but also in the one to come" (1:21).

To understand this more fully, note Paul's description of Jesus Christ in the Philippian letter. In this passage, he tells us that Jesus was "in very nature God." However, He "did not consider equality with God something to be grasped." He was willing to make "himself nothing, taking the very nature of a servant." He was actually "made in human likeness." It was in this form—the form of a man—that "he humbled himself and became obedient to death—even death on a cross!" (Phil. 2:6-8)

However, Jesus Christ did not remain a dead man. The mighty power of God was released and He came forth from the tomb on the third day. And then, once again "God exalted him to the *highest place* and gave him *the name* that is above every name, that at the name of Jesus every knee should bow, in heaven and on earth and under the earth, and every tongue confess that Jesus Christ is Lord, to the glory of God the Father" (2:9-11).

Inherent in this passage are some incredible realities. For Christ to be "in very nature God" means that He was one with God. In fact, the Apostle John tells us that Jesus Christ "was God," and "through Him all things were made" (John 1:1,3). Thus when He was once again exalted "to the highest place" and given "the name that is above every name," He was simply reinstated to His former position—only this time as our great High Priest and Mediator who had provided for our eternal salvation.

Furthermore, "God placed all things under his feet and appointed him to be head over everything for the church, which is his body, the fullness of him who fills everything in every way" (Eph. 1:22).

With this statement, Paul seemed to be saying that the Church of Jesus Christ was and is God's greatest and glorious creation and the ultimate in demonstrating His "incomparable" power. It was this power that provided redemption in Christ through His resurrection and ascension. And this leads us to the application of God's power on our behalf.

GOD'S POWER APPLIED

Paul goes on to drive home the point that God's power was

indeed released on our behalf. Speaking to the Ephesians before their conversion, he said: "As for you, you were *dead* in your transgressions and sins . . . . But because of his great love for us, God, who is rich in mercy, *made us alive in Christ* even when *we were dead* in transgressions . . . . God raised us up with Christ and seated us with him in the heavenly realms in Christ Jesus" (2:1,4-6).

In this context we can understand more fully Paul's first two requests on behalf of the Ephesian Christians. First, he kept asking the Lord to enlighten their hearts so that they might know God better. A significant part of that "knowledge" involves understanding "God's incomparably great power" in saving us.

Second, Paul prayed that their hearts might be enlightened in order that they might know "the hope to which he has called" them. With this specific request he wanted them to know God's incomparable power in not only providing for their salvation, but in making that salvation secure. It is the basis of our hope.

HOW SHOULD THESE GREAT TRUTHS AFFECT US?

The knowledge of God's power should cause us to be secure in Christ. This is precisely what Peter had in mind in his first letter when he wrote: "Praise be to the God and Father of our Lord Jesus Christ! In his great mercy he has given us new birth into a *living hope* through the *resurrection* of Jesus Christ from the dead, and into *an inheritance* that can never perish, spoil or fade—kept in heaven for you, who through faith are *shielded by God's power* until the coming of the salvation that is ready to be revealed in the last time" (1 Pet. 1:3-5).

Here Peter was saying the same thing Paul was praying about on behalf of the Ephesian Christians. It is *God's power* that is shielding and protecting our eternal inheritance.

A knowledge of God's power should be reassuring in the midst of pressure and problems. David Livingston had spent 16 years in Africa, but all during that time he faced extreme danger on only one occasion. He was surrounded by hostile, angry natives in the heart of Africa. He was in danger of losing his life and contemplated fleeing in the night. But something happened that changed his mind and gave him peace in his perilous situation. He recorded it in his diary on January 14, 1856:

> I felt much turmoil of spirit in prospect of having all my plans for the welfare of this great region and this teeming population knocked on the head by savages tomorrow. But I read that Jesus said: *"All power* is given unto Me in heaven and in earth. Go ye therefore and teach all nations, and lo, I am with you always, even unto the end of the world." It is the word of a gentleman of the most strict and sacred honor, so there is an end to it! I will not cross furtively tonight as I intended. Should such a man as I flee? Nay, verily, I shall take observations for latitude and longitude tonight, though they may be the last. I feel quite calm now, thank God!

Like the Apostle Paul, David Livingston understood the power of God. Whether by life or by death, he was willing to face the unknown. No matter what happened, he knew he would be delivered, either to continue with his ministry or to be taken home to heaven and set totally free. In God's providence, of course, He gave David Livingston divine protection for continued ministry on this earth; but for the Apostle Paul, He soon took him home to heaven. The Christian cannot lose. For "if God be for us, who can be against us?" God's power will be experienced on our behalf whether in life or in death. In some respects His power is greater in death than in preserving our life on earth, for it relates directly to the power demonstrated in the resurrection and ascension of Christ.

The knowledge of God's power should humble us. At the funeral of Louis XIV, the great cathedral was packed with mourners paying final tribute to the king whom they all considered great. The room was dark, except for one lone candle that illumined the great solid casket which held the mortal remains of the monarch.

At the appointed time, Massilion, the court preacher, stood to address the assembled clergy of France. As he rose, he reached over the pulpit and snuffed out the one candle that was there to symbolize the greatness of the king. Then from the darkness came just four words: "God *only* is great."

A true knowledge of God's power and human arrogance are incompatible. To know God in this way inevitably creates humility. Don't misunderstand! This does not mean weakness! God has shared some of His power with mankind, for we are capable of accomplishing some great things. But all that we can *ever* accomplish is minute and infinitesimal compared with God's accomplishments. A true knowledge of God makes that point clear to every thinking human being. All that we are and have and all we can do is because of *His* power—not ours!

The knowledge of God's power should turn our hearts toward Christ for our salvation. C. H. Robinson tells the story of Jonathan Edwards, the great theologian and preacher, who was suddenly converted as if in a flash of light. It happened when he was reading a single verse from the New Testament. He was at home in his father's house while the rest of the family went to church. During those hours at home with nothing to do, he listlessly went into the library. On the shelf he saw a leather-backed volume that evoked his curiosity. When he opened it, he found it to be the Bible and his eye fell on this verse: "Now unto the King eternal, immortal, invisible, the only wise God, be honor and glory forever and ever. Amen!"

Jonathan Edwards recorded in his journal that the immediate effect of this verse was awakening and alarming to his soul. He thought immediately of the vastness and majesty of the true Sovereign of the universe. Out of this knowledge grew the pain of guilt for having resisted such a Monarch so long and for having served Him so poorly. Before, he understood just a little of his own sinful nature and felt little remorse for his sin. However, catching a glimpse of the greatness of God brought him to a state of deep contrition. He accepted Christ as his Saviour, realizing for the first time the power that God had revealed in Christ on his behalf.

Earlier I shared the story of Mount St. Helens and Mount Krakatoa. But these demonstrations of power are nothing compared with the power that will be released someday on sinful humanity. It will be beyond anything man has ever seen or experienced. It will happen during that period of time known as the Great Tribulation—those dreadful days when God will pour out His wrath on an unrepentant, sinful humanity. Read the Apostle John's report in the book of Revelation: "The seventh angel poured out his bowl into the air, and out of the temple came a loud voice from the throne, saying, 'It is done!' Then there came flashes of lightning, rumblings, peals of thunder and a *severe earthquake. No earthquake like it has ever occurred* since man has been on earth, so tremendous was the quake. The great city split into three parts, and *the cities of the nations collapsed.* God remembered Babylon the Great and gave her the cup filled with the wine of the fury of his wrath. *Every island fled away* and the *mountains could not be found.* From the sky huge *hailstones* of about a hundred pounds each fell upon men" (Rev. 16:17-21).

What is amazing is that John goes on to report that during this great period of catastrophe, men still "cursed God" (v. 16).

Today, we live in the day of grace. God is still calling for men to repent. He is longsuffering and patient, "not wanting anyone to perish, but everyone to come to repentance" (2 Pet. 3:9). However, Peter wrote, "The day of the Lord *will come* like a thief. The heavens will disappear with a roar; the elements will be destroyed by fire, and the earth and everything in it will be laid bare" (3:10).

If you are a Christian, you need not fear God's power. You can rejoice in that power. So, if you're feeling down, look up! In Christ you are already seated with Christ in the heavenly realms!

Note

1. Excerpt from EPHESIANS 1-3 (*Anchor Bible*) translated and edited by Markus Barth. Copyright © 1974 by Doubleday & Company, Inc. Reprinted by permission of the publisher.

8

Understanding God's Grace

EPHESIANS 2:1-10

As for you, you were dead in your transgressions and sins, in which you used to live when you followed the ways of this world and of the ruler of the kingdom of the air, the spirit who is now at work in those who are disobedient. All of us also lived among them at one time, gratifying the cravings of our sinful nature and following its desires and thoughts. Like the rest, we were by nature objects of wrath. But because of his great love for us, God, who is rich in mercy, made us alive with Christ even when we were dead in transgressions—it is by grace you have been saved. And God raised us up with Christ and seated us with him in the heavenly realms in Christ Jesus, in order that in the coming ages he might show the incomparable riches of his grace, expressed in his kindness to us in Christ Jesus. For it is by grace you have been saved, through faith—and this not from yourselves, it is the gift of God—not by works, so that no one can boast. For we are God's workmanship, created in Christ Jesus to do good works, which God prepared in advance for us to do.

In thinking about the subject of "grace," I could not help but recall an incident in my own life. Following an appointment I had with a member of our church, I was driving my car back to my office and suddenly noticed a police car behind me. I immediately looked down at my speedometer and breathed a sigh of relief when I saw I was not breaking the speed limit.

A few blocks later, since we were on a four-lane street, the policeman pulled his car up beside me. And so, we traveled together, side by side, for about a mile. Periodically I glanced at him and I could see that he was looking back at me. I could also see another man sitting beside him in the front seat—which somewhat aroused my curiosity. But I *knew* I wasn't breaking the law, so I was pretty relaxed—in fact, a bit proud of myself for having maintained the speed limit.

Finally, I pulled up to a main expressway. After making the turn, I decided to stay on the service road, while the policeman pulled out onto the main highway. Again we traveled side-by-side—he on the expressway and I on the service road. And again we periodically glanced at each other.

To my surprise, however, after coming to the next exit, the policeman pulled off the main road, came in behind me and turned on his flashing light. Since we had been keeping such good visual communication all along, I saw the light immediately and pulled to an abrupt stop. He got out of his car, walked up to my window—which I had rolled down—and cordially introduced himself. He asked for my driver's license, checked it out, and then proceeded to outline for me some observations that left me speechless.

"Sir," he said in a very polite fashion, "back on the road before we turned onto the main highway, you failed to make a complete stop at . . . . " and then he named a particular street. My wife would have called it one of my famous "rolling stops," if you know what I mean. "That's violation number one," said the officer.

"Furthermore," he continued, "when you reached the main expressway, you failed to observe the yield sign. That's violation number two." By then my jaw was beginning to drop! I couldn't believe what I was hearing.

"Also," he continued, "when we were traveling side-by-side, you on the service road and I on the highway, you were over the speed limit on the service road. That's violation number three." By then the blood was beginning to drain from my face.

But the officer wasn't through! "And finally," he said, pointing to my windshield, "your inspection sticker is overdue! That's violation number four." At that point I wished I had an ejection seat or some "invisibility pills" to be able to retreat from that man's presence. My embarrassment was overwhelming.

"However," the officer continued, after a brief pause, giving me a moment to recover from what he probably thought was a cardiac arrest, "I have a fugitive with me," he said, pointing back to his squad car. "I have to get him to the station immediately and don't have time to write out a ticket. But I wanted to warn you. Good day," he said with a smile. "And do be careful!" He then got in his car and went on his way.

I sat there for a few moments, trying to recap in my own thinking what was going through my head when I, in full view of that police officer, proceeded to flagrantly and consistently violate the law. I was totally unaware of my own unlawful acts—in fact, quite secure in what I thought was righteous behavior.

Once I cleared my head, and again began to breathe normally, I came to one basic conclusion: "That, Gene Getz, is an illustration of pure grace—pure, unadulterated grace. That man could have thrown the book at you." The facts are, of course, he probably could have taken me down to the station and made me post bond which would have looked really nice in the newspaper. In my mind's eye I could see the headline: "Pastor guilty of four violations in full view of police officer."

I'm not proud of this incident, but I wanted to share it with you because it *does* illustrate, to a certain extent at least, the biblical concept of grace. John MacArthur, in one of his messages, states that "the word 'grace' literally means undeserved, unrecompensed kindness. It means mercy. It is not some little ingratiated act. It is super-magnanimous, for it is undeserved. And it cannot be paid back. Grace, always in Scripture, has to be a free gift, unearned."[1]

The Apostle Paul in the next section of his letter to the

Ephesians, focuses on the subject of grace. His thoughts can be developed around three basic questions.

WHO ARE THE *RECIPIENTS* OF GOD'S GRACE?

"As for *you*, *you* were dead in your transgressions and sins, in which *you* used to live when *you* followed the ways of this world and of the ruler of the kingdom of the air, the spirit who is now at work in those who are disobedient" (Eph. 2:1-2).

Who was Paul speaking to in these verses when he used the word "you"? In order to answer this question adequately, we need to look more carefully at the context. In fact, to this point in this letter Paul had already made several subtle shifts regarding his audience without specifically identifying them. After addressing the saints in Ephesus and probably in the surrounding area (1:1-2), Paul referred to both Jews and Gentiles who had come to Christ.

Believing Jews and Gentiles

In the following statements the italicized pronouns refer to every person who would read this letter who had come to Jesus Christ, whether Jew or Gentile.

- "For he chose *us*" (1:4).
- "In love he predestined *us*" (1:5).
- "In him *we* have redemption" (1:7).
- "He lavished [His grace] on *us*" (1:8).
- "He made known to *us* the mystery of his will" (1:9).

Believing Jews

In verse 11 Paul shifted his emphasis to believing Jews. He wrote: "In him *we* were *also* chosen, having been predestined according to the plan of him who works out everything in conformity with the purpose of his will, in order that *we, who* were the *first to hope in Christ,* might be for the praise of his glory" (Eph. 1:11-12).

Here Paul was speaking specifically about Jews who had come to Christ, including himself. The first Christians were "Jewish" Christians. When we understand this shift in emphasis we can understand what appears to be repetition in Paul's opening paragraph. In reality it is purposeful repetition, for Paul was emphasizing that he and other Jews had also been "chosen" and "predestined" in God's great plan and they were among those who had been the *"first* to hope in Christ." This, of course, is verified in the Gospels and in the opening section of the book of Acts. Jesus Christ, a Jew, came first to His own people, and when the Church was born, the Holy Spirit first came upon the Jews who had gathered in Jerusalem. The Jerusalem church was a Jewish church.

Believing Gentiles

Paul shifted his emphasis again in verse 13 directing his thoughts to the main recipients of this letter—Gentiles who had come to Christ. Thus we read: "And *you also* were included in Christ when *you* heard the word of truth, the gospel of your salvation. Having believed, *you* were marked in him with a seal, the promised Holy Spirit" (Eph. 1:13).

Now Paul was directing his thoughts to those people Jesus called "other sheep" (John 10:16). He was speaking to Gentiles who had also heard the gospel, responded to "the word of truth," and experienced the same thing the Jews had experienced in Jerusalem on the day of Pentecost (Acts 2:1-11).

Believing Jews and Gentiles

As Paul concluded this opening paragraph in his letter to the Ephesians, he once again shifted his emphasis and included both Jews and Gentiles in verse 14. The Holy Spirit, he wrote, "is a deposit guaranteeing *our* inheritance [both those of us 'who were the *first* to hope in Christ' as well as 'you also' who were included in Christ]" (1:14).

Believing Gentiles

From this point forward in chapter 1, the "you" and "your" pronouns refer basically to those Gentiles who responded to the gospel in Ephesus and the surrounding area. The prayer we have just studied (Eph. 1:15-23) and the three major requests were for these people. And as we come to chapter 2, verse 1,

Paul is still continuing to direct his thoughts to these Gentile converts. Thus when we read: "As for *you, you* were dead in *your* transgressions and sins" he was referring to the Gentile believers who had been "included in Christ" when they had heard "the word of truth."

Believing Jews and Gentiles

Paul does not expand his audience again until verse 3. At that time, however, he once again included all believers, both Jews and Gentiles. Thus we read: "*All of us* also lived among them [that is, the unsaved Gentiles] at one time, gratifying the cravings of *our* sinful nature and following its desires and thoughts. Like the rest we [unsaved Jews] were by nature objects of wrath."

Who then are the *recipients* of God's grace? The answer is clear. Anyone who has experienced salvation in Jesus Christ is a recipient of God's grace. When Jews are saved they are saved by God's grace. When Gentiles are saved they also are saved by God's grace. And so every category of human being who has ever been saved was saved by God's grace.

Interestingly, Paul greatly expanded this concept in the first three chapters of his letter to the Romans. After giving convincing evidence that both Jew and Gentile are under condemnation, he concluded by saying, "There is no difference, for *all* have sinned and fall short of the glory of God, and are justified freely by his *grace* through the redemption that came by Christ Jesus" (Rom. 3:22-24).

WHAT ARE THE *REASONS* FOR GOD'S GRACE?

In the next four verses, Paul gave at least three reasons *why* God has made His grace available to *all* mankind.

God's Love

The first reason is God's unconditional and unfathomable love. Paul identified it in this passage as God's "great love." Thus we read: "But because of his *great love for us,* God . . . made us alive with Christ even when we were dead in transgressions" (Eph. 2:4,5).

Jesus Himself said, "For God so loved the world that he gave his one and only Son, that whoever believes in him shall not perish but have eternal life" (John 3:16).

God's Mercy

Paul states another reason in verse 4, for the grace He has bestowed on us—His mercy. Proceeding from love, this reason indicates that God has taken pity on sinful mankind. He is merciful. Thus we read: "But because of his great love for us, God, who is *is rich in mercy,* made us alive with Christ even when we were dead in transgressions" (Eph. 2:4,5). God's loving actions toward us are not just an act of the will, a choice that is void of feelings. It involves emotions. God has compassion on us.

This attribute of God was dramatically illustrated when Jesus came to Bethany following the death of His friend Lazarus. Mary, Lazarus's sister, was deeply distressed and was weeping. "Lord," she said, "if you had been here, my brother would not have died" (John 11:32).

John records that "when Jesus saw her weeping, and the Jews who had come along with her also weeping, he was *deeply moved* in spirit and troubled" (11:33). Jesus then asked where they had laid him, and as He went to the tomb, "Jesus wept" (11:35).

Those who were looking on immediately recognized why Jesus was weeping. Thus they said, "See how he *loved him!*" (11:36). Jesus had mercy on His friends and on Lazarus and raised this man from the dead.

God's Kindness

There's an interesting correlation between the raising of Lazarus and what God has done for us. In Ephesians 2:6-7 we read that "God raised us up with Christ and seated us with him in the heavenly realms in Christ Jesus, in order that in the coming ages he might show the incomparable riches of his grace, expressed in his *kindness* to us in Christ Jesus."

God's mercy towards us focuses on His compassion. God's "kindness" towards us focuses on His love in action.

Jesus dramatically illustrated this quality when He told the story of the Good Samaritan. As you remember, the man was traveling from Jerusalem to Jericho and was attacked by robbers. They tore off his clothes, beat him and left him half dead. First, a priest was traveling on the road but passed by on the other side. Next a Levite came by and when he saw him he also moved over to the other side of the road. But then a Samaritan approached the scene of this tragic event. Jesus said, "When he saw him, he took *pity* on him" (Luke 10:33). That's *mercy!*

But we go on to read that the Samaritan "went to him and bandaged his wounds, pouring on oil and wine. Then he put the man on his own donkey, took him to an inn and took care of him" (10:34). And the next morning when he left the inn, he gave the proprietor some money. "Look after him," he said, "and when I return, I will reimburse you for any extra expense you may have" (10:35). That, you see, is *kindness*—love in action.

In a beautiful way the story of the Good Samaritan illustrates all of the reasons God made His grace available to mankind. The source of His divine grace is His unconditional *love* which has been demonstrated by His compassionate *mercy* and unselfish *kindness*.

WHAT ARE THE *RESULTS* OF GOD'S GRACE?

As Paul culminates this paragraph on the grace of God, he spells out two results.

God's Gift of Salvation

In this paragraph we have two of the most explicit and yet misunderstood verses in the New Testament. Paul wrote, "For it is by grace you have been saved, through faith—and this not from yourselves, it is the gift of God—not by works, so that no one can boast" (Eph. 2:8-9).

This is not the first time Paul referred to the grace of God in this letter as it relates to our salvation. In chapter 1, verse 6 Paul identified this quality as God's *"glorious grace,* which he has *freely given* us in the One he loves."* Paul continued by saying that in Christ "we have redemption through his blood, the forgiveness of sins, in accordance with the *riches of God's grace* that he lavished on us with all wisdom and understanding" (1:7-8).

Salvation is a gift. It cannot be earned. There is nothing we can do to pay for it. It can only be received by faith.

Salvation by grace through faith is what separates true Christianity from all other religions as well as all cults and isms that are deviations from biblical Christianity. Without exception, all teach "salvation by works" or a combination of "faith and works."

Have you ever shared the gospel with someone who has responded by saying that all religions are basically the same? Generally speaking, that view is correct—with one exception. The Bible teaches that man is saved by God's grace through faith, not by works, whereas most other religions teach that man is saved by works or by faith plus works. Consequently, a person who has been exposed to the majority of religions in the world *does* see that similarity. Unfortunately, he has not understood this basic truth about *true* Christianity.

A Christian's Good Works

Where then do works fit in? Paul made that very clear in verse 10 when he said, "For we are God's workmanship, created in Christ Jesus *to do good works,* which God prepared in advance for us to do" (Eph. 2:10).

With this statement Paul was saying that true conversion results in "good works." In fact, this is God's plan. Furthermore, anyone who truly understands and has experienced the grace of God responds to the grace of God.

The true test, then, of whether or not we have experienced the grace of God is the effect it has on our lives. The Scriptures make it clear that true faith results in good works. In fact, as James wrote, "Faith without deeds is dead" (James 2:26). If we are truly saved, God's grace will also cause us to conform our lives to the life of Jesus Christ.

HOW SHOULD WE *RESPOND* TO GOD'S GRACE?

This passage of Scripture poses two questions for every human being.

1. *Have I responded to God's love, mercy and kindness and*

*experienced God's grace by receiving through faith His free
gift of salvation?*

To help you think more deeply about this question, consider
for a moment my experience with the police officer. I was totally
surprised when he pulled me over and outlined for me in clear
and succinct fashion that I was guilty of violating four laws, one
right after the other. I actually thought I was keeping the law. In
fact, I felt rather self-righteous as I was driving along beside the
squad car. However, the fact that I thought I wasn't breaking the
law did not mean I wasn't guilty. Furthermore, in one instance I
was ignorant of the law—specifically the actual speed limit on
the service road. But I was guilty nevertheless. You see, ignorance of the law is no excuse!

The same situation applies to millions of people today who
are violating God's laws. Some people feel they are doing a good
job keeping the Ten Commandments. They actually believe they
are righteous before God. However, the Bible teaches that if we
violate just one commandment at any moment, we are just as
guilty as if we violated all of them (Jas. 2:10). God cannot look
upon *any* sin. That is why Jesus Christ came as the perfect Son
of God and took our sins upon Himself at the cross.

So, if you are trying to get to heaven by keeping the law,
you'll never make it. No one except Jesus Christ Himself kept
the law perfectly. That is why He was the perfect Saviour. The
only way to have eternal life is to acknowledge your sin and
receive Jesus Christ as personal Saviour and then receive the
free gift of salvation.

Note something else regarding my experience with the
police officer. When he informed me that he was not going to
write out a ticket, what if I had responded by saying, "Sir, I'm
not going to accept your offer of freedom. I'm guilty of breaking
the law. Book me! Fine me! Put me behind bars!"

I'm sure you'll agree that I would have been very foolish to
reject this offer. It wouldn't make sense.

But neither does it make sense to reject God's offer of salvation. And yet, millions of people are responding to the gospel by
saying, "Bring judgment on me; make me pay for my sins; put
me behind bars—forever!"

True, many people are not aware of the plan of salvation. Many do not understand that the gift is free. But many do know the truth yet refuse to respond positively to God's offer. This, of course, does not make sense. It is a very foolish decision.

And so, if you know the truth—and if you've read to this point, you certainly do know the truth—don't force God to bring judgment upon you. Accept His free gift of salvation. As the Bible states: *"Today*, if you hear his voice, do not harden your hearts"* (Heb. 4:7).

>   2. *If you are a Christian, are you allowing God's grace to teach you and to conform you to the image of His Son Jesus Christ?*

A number of years ago now, I was living in Billings, Montana, going to college and participating in the ministry as well. Periodically I made the 1,600-mile trip by train between Chicago and Billings. Consequently, I had a lot of time to read. On one trip I read a book entitled *Disciplined by Grace* by J. F. Strombeck. The book was actually an explanation of Paul's words to Titus: "For the *grace of God* that brings salvation has appeared to all men. It *teaches us* to say "No" to ungodliness and worldly passions, and to live self-controlled, upright and godly lives in this present age, while we wait for the blessed hope—the glorious appearing of our great God and Savior, Jesus Christ, who gave himself for us to redeem us from all wickedness and to purify for himself a people that are his very own, eager to do what is good" (Titus 2:11-14).

You'll note that "grace" not only brings salvation to the non-Christian, but it also teaches the Christian. The truth in these verses, as explained by Mr. Strombeck, was life-changing for me, particularly in view of my own legalistic religious background. I saw that a true knowledge and experience of God's grace would impact a Christian's life far more significantly than a set of rules. Strombeck summarizes this reality with the following statement:

>   It is not only important to know the meaning of grace; it is equally necessary to realize the extent to which grace enters into the believer's life. This is

essential as a background for understanding the discipline of grace.

Many think of grace merely as the means whereby God forgives sin; and fail to recognize that grace is God's way of dealing with one who receives Christ, not only during the earthly existence, but also throughout eternity. Great harm has come from this limited conception of grace and the lack of teaching the fulness thereof. The present low level of Christian conduct is largely due to incomplete teaching of grace. All misconceptions on the part of many, that an over-emphasis on grace is a license to sin, would quickly be removed if grace were preached and understood in its fullness.[3]

And so, every Christian should ask himself the question, Am I allowing God's grace, with which He saved me, to also teach me to live a Christian life in this world?

Notes

1. Used by permission of Dr. John MacArthur.
2. Taken from: DISCIPLINED BY GRACE by J. F. Strombeck. Copyright © 1982 Harvest House Publishers, 1075 Arrowsmith, Eugene, OR 97402. Used by permission.

9

Understanding
Our Oneness In Christ

EPHESIANS 2:11-22

Therefore, remember that formerly you who are Gentiles by birth and called "uncircumcised" by those who call themselves "the circumcision" (that done in the body by the hands of men)— remember that at that time you were separate from Christ, excluded from citizenship in Israel and foreigners to the covenants of the promise, without hope and without God in the world. But now in Christ Jesus you who once were far away have been brought near through the blood of Christ.

For he himself is our peace, who has made the two one and has destroyed the barrier, the dividing wall of hostility, by abolishing in his flesh the law with its commandments and regulations. His purpose was to create in himself one new man out of the two, thus making peace, and in this one body to reconcile both of them to God through the cross, by which he put to death their hostility. He came and preached peace to you who were far away and peace to those who were near. For through him we both have access to the Father by one Spirit.

Consequently, you are no longer foreigners and aliens, but fellow citizens with God's people and members of God's household, built on the foundation of the apostles and prophets, with Christ Jesus himself as the chief cornerstone. In him the whole building is joined together and rises to become a holy temple in the Lord. And in him you too are being built together to become a dwelling in which God lives by his Spirit.

All of us at some point in time have been guilty of prejudice, that is, looking down on others and thinking we are better than someone else without a logical and reasonable basis for our reactions. It might be related to social class and economics. It might reflect religious attitudes. It might be racial or ethnic in origin. In fact, most if not all of us have elements of prejudice and social pride that we don't even recognize in ourselves.

No prejudice, however, has ever run deeper and reflected more hostility and lasted longer than that which has permeated Jewish and Gentile communities throughout the centuries. Emotions have often run high on both sides, and still do in many parts of the world. Though anti-Semitic attitudes and behavior have become a common theme in newspapers and magazines, on radio and television, *mutual* hostility and resentment are obvious.

Paul, while reminding the Ephesians that Jesus Christ has made it possible to change all of this, also deals with the reality of this deep racial and religious phenomenon. Directing his thoughts first to believing Gentiles, he reminds them of their status before they put their faith in Jesus Christ. But before he outlines their position outside of Christ, Paul establishes an historical background in verse 11 of chapter 2.

First, they were "Gentiles by birth." In actuality this takes us back to the beginning of the human race. Gentiles have their origin in Adam. Following the Fall, the whole world was plunged into sin. In fact, mankind became so evil and corrupt that God decided to put an end to all people (Gen. 6:5-8, 11-13). And so He did, with the exception of Noah and his family. Because of this man's righteous life-style and relationship with Him, God preserved Noah and his children from the flood (6:8-10).

Following the flood, the people who emerged from Noah's family line once again turned against God. Paul described this dismal situation in his letter to the Romans: "For although they knew God, they neither glorified him as God nor gave thanks to him, but their thinking became futile and their foolish hearts were darkened" (Rom. 1:21).

During this time of human deterioration, people actually "exchanged the glory of the immortal God for images made to look like mortal *men* and *birds* and *animals* and *reptiles*" (1:23). Note mankind's spiritual and moral deterioration. Men and women moved from worshiping God to worshiping themselves and then to lower forms of animals.

But God in His mercy did not turn His back on mankind, though *all* people had turned their backs on God (3:23). He reached down in love and chose first a man (Abraham) and then a nation (Israel) to whom He wanted to reveal His love and to draw many people back to Himself. He made a covenant with Abraham, promising him a land, a seed and a blessing. God's ultimate plan was that "all peoples of the earth" would "be blessed" through Abraham's seed (Gen. 12:1-3). That seed was Jesus Christ.

The Jews, then, have their origin in Abraham. They were first called "Hebrews" (Gen. 14:13; 40:15). Later they were called "Israelites," after God changed Jacob's name to Israel (32:28).

Following the Babylonian captivity, the title "Jew", originally used to describe the tribe of Judah, was used of all Israel. Generally, the term "Israel" was used to refer to these people as a *nation*, whereas the term "Jew" was used to designate the *people* themselves. The same is true today.

Second, the Gentiles were an uncircumcised people. When Abraham was 99 years old, God confirmed the eternal covenant of circumcision which He had made with this servant years earlier. "Every male among you shall be circumcised," God said (Gen. 17:10). And the Lord made it clear that this "sign of the covenant" (17:11) should be practiced for "generations to come" (17:12).

And so it was, through the years, that circumcision became the distinguishing factor between Jews and Gentiles. Thus Paul wrote that "Gentiles by birth" were "called 'uncircumcised' by those who call themselves 'the circumcision'" (Eph. 2:11). And to make sure that his readers knew he was talking about the physical act of circumcision, not just a spiritual idea, Paul added, "that done in the body by hands of men" (Eph. 2:11).

THE STATUS OF UNSAVED GENTILES

Paul next asked his readers (believing Gentiles) to "remember" (Eph. 2:12) their former status as unbelieving Gentiles. He outlines their condition with five succinct but very descriptive phrases. They were:

- "Separate from Christ"
- "Excluded from citizenship in Israel"
- "Foreigners to the covenants of the promise"
- "Without hope"
- Without God in the world" (2:12).

Paul was not saying that Gentiles could not come to know God. Rather, he was stating a condition. Remember that all mankind had chosen to follow evil rather than good. Even Abraham was a pagan. He too worshiped false gods. But the *true God* chose this man out of his paganism to be a means to provide salvation for those who would respond to His love and grace. The nation Israel was to be a corporate witness of God's righteousness in this world. Unfortunately, in the most part they failed utterly to fulfill this commission. And so the great majority of Gentiles continued in their lost condition before Christ came.

Note also that being a Jew by calling did not make God's chosen people true believers. In fact, when Christ came, the great majority of Jews were also unbelievers. Though they believed in God, claimed to keep the law, and were even circumcised, they were not God's children spiritually. Paul made this crystal clear in his letter to the Romans when he wrote: "A man is not a Jew if he is only one outwardly, nor is circumcision merely outward and physical. No, a man is a Jew if he is one inwardly; and circumcision is circumcision of the heart, by the Spirit, not by the written code. Such a man's praise is not from men, but from God" (Rom. 2:28-29).

The same can be said of people who claim to be Christians today. They claim to follow Christ and have even been baptized. However, many of these people have not really been born again by God's Spirit. Their Christianity is purely ritualistic. They belong to the institutional church, but they do not belong to Christ. They are practicing "churchianity," not Christianity.

THE STATUS OF SAVED JEWS *AND* GENTILES

The fact that both Jews and Gentiles needed salvation—and still do today—leads to Paul's next section in his letter. Here he included himself and all Israel. Once again Paul broadened his audience. Rather than using the pronoun "you" to refer to believing Gentiles who would receive this letter, he used the pronoun "our" to refer to both believing Jews and Gentiles. His focus was Christ and what happened at the cross:

- Jesus Christ "is *our* peace".
- Jesus Christ "has made the two one"
- Jesus Christ "has destroyed the barrier, the dividing wall of hostility"
- Jesus Christ abolished "in his flesh the law with its commandments and regulations"
- Jesus Christ created "in himself one new man out of the two"
- Jesus Christ reconciled *both* Jews and Gentiles "to God through the cross"
- Jesus Christ "preached peace" to the Gentiles "who were far away"
- Jesus Christ "preached peace" to the Jews "who were near"
- Jesus Christ made it possible for *both* Jew and Gentile to have "access to the Father by one Spirit" (Eph. 2:14-18).

The primary thrust in this paragraph describing the fact that both Jew and Gentile can be saved through Christ's work on the cross is that there should no longer be a division between these two groups of people. They are *one* in Christ. The barriers that have grown up over the years, and the horrible hostility that has existed leading to some of the most terrible atrocities, should no longer exist among Christians.

Note too that Paul is not saying that Jesus Christ eliminated or destroyed the Law of Moses (2:15). Rather, He fulfilled the law. He paid the ultimate price for sin that the law demanded. He died on the cross. In this sense, the law is no longer necessary as a means to point to Christ's sacrifice.

Neither is it necessary to keep all of the legalistic aspects of the law in order to have a proper relationship with God. The moral aspects of the law, as they are embodied in the Ten Commandments, of course, are ongoing. With the exception of ritualistically keeping the Sabbath day, all of the commandments are repeated and emphasized for Christians in the New Testament. Furthermore, Christians are given a divine means by which we can progressively conform our lives to God's commandments. This is what Paul had in mind in his Roman letter when he wrote: "Therefore, there is now no condemnation for those who are in Christ Jesus, because through Christ Jesus the law of the Spirit of life set me free from the law of sin and death. For what the law was powerless to do in that it was weakened by the sinful nature, God did by sending his own Son in the likeness of sinful man to be a sin offering. And so he condemned sin in sinful man, in order that *the righteous requirements of the law might be fully met in us,* who do not live according to the sinful nature, but according to the Spirit" (Rom. 8:1-4).

THE STATUS OF SAVED GENTILES

In this final paragraph in Ephesians 2, Paul redirected his thoughts once again to his readers, speaking to those who were believing Gentiles. He actually began his profile with his transitional statement in verse 13:

- "You who were once far away have been brought near through the blood of Christ."
- "You are no longer foreigners and aliens"
- You are "fellow citizens with God's people"
- You are "members of God's household"
- You are "built on the foundation of the apostles and prophets, with Christ Jesus himself as the chief cornerstone."
- You are "built together to become a dwelling in which God lives by his Spirit" (Eph. 2:13,19-21).

It is true that the first church was a Jewish church. The original apostles and prophets were also Jews. But this was just the beginning point. It was God's plan that both Jews and Gentiles make up the Church and that there be no continuing division.

Unfortunately it took time for even the apostles to recognize this truth. Their prejudice was so deeply ingrained that it took a special act of God to get this point across, which is dramatically illustrated in the book of Acts. In fact, all that Paul stated in his Ephesian letter is illustrated and "fleshed out" in the story of Peter's encounter with Cornelius.

A BIBLICAL ILLUSTRATION

Some time after the founding of the Church in Jerusalem, Peter was in Joppa. On that day he went up to pray on the roof of the house where he was staying. During this time of prayer, Peter "became hungry." While a meal was being prepared below, he "fell into a trance" (Acts 10:10) and saw a most unusual vision. Heaven opened and a large sheet descended, held by its four corners, and filled with all kinds of animals. Then Peter heard a voice: "Get up, Peter. Kill and eat" (10:13).

Peter resisted since, as a Jew, he had never eaten any animals classified in the law as "unclean," and the sheet included some of those animals. But three times the voice instructed Peter to eat and not to "call anything impure that God has made clean" (10:15).

Peter couldn't understand what was happening. But in the meantime, God had spoken to Cornelius, a Gentile who lived in Caesarea. Cornelius had been worshiping God and seeking to do His will. One afternoon he too had a vision. An angel of the Lord appeared to him and told him to look for Peter in Joppa.

To make a long story short, Cornelius sent three men to find Peter. When they arrived in Joppa, Peter's heart was already prepared through his own vision. The next day he traveled to Caesarea to meet with Cornelius and his family. When he entered the house Peter made it very clear that in his mind "the dividing wall of hostility" still existed. He stated, "You are well aware that it is against our law for a Jew to associate with a Gentile" (10:28). This statement demonstrates clearly the extent to which the Jews had perverted God's original intent in giving the law.

However, when Peter heard Cornelius's full story, he took a

giant step forward in understanding and accepting God's redemptive plan of salvation. He told Cornelius, "I now realize how true it is that *God does not show favoritism,* but accepts men from every nation who fear him and do what is right. This is the message God sent to the people of Israel, telling the good news of peace through Jesus Christ, who is *Lord of all*" (10:34-36).

Peter had heard this truth before from the lips of Jesus Christ Himself. But he evidently did not believe it or accept it in his heart. He was a staunch and prejudiced Jew who had been saturated with Hebrew tradition. As with Saul, it took a dramatic event, a revelation of God, to convince him that God cared about Gentiles and had provided for their salvation.

The Jews who accompanied Peter on this mission also had to come to grips with their prejudice. In fact, we read that "the circumcised believers who came with Peter were astonished that the gift of the Holy Spirit had been poured out even on the Gentiles" (10:45), even as He came upon the Jews in Jerusalem on the day of Pentecost.

When Peter returned to Jerusalem he shared what had happened. However, he faced a wall of continuing prejudice. "The circumcised believers criticized him and said, 'You went into the house of uncircumcised men and ate with them'" (11:2-3).

However, as Peter related the story, their prejudiced attitudes and feelings began to dissipate. They finally acknowledged, "So then, God has [would you believe] *even granted* the Gentiles repentance unto life" (11:18). It is obvious that they acknowledged the facts with their heads, but they were still having problems with their hearts. And so it is with prejudice. It often lingers and is so subtle that we don't even recognize it as being a part of our lives.

WHAT ABOUT YOU?

There are two dimensions to prejudice that every human being and particularly every Christian should come to grips with.

The Problem of Inferiority

There are some who have become so victimized by people in

their circumstances of life that they have concluded that God does not really love them—at least, not as much as He does others! This is a special problem among people who feel that they have failed God so utterly that He could never accept them.

This is uniquely illustrated when Jesus talked with the woman at the well near Sychar, a city in Samaria. Interestingly, this story begins: "Now he [Jesus] *had to go* through Samaria" (John 4:4). With this historical statement, the Apostle John was telling us that it was unusual for Jesus to take this route, for Jews simply did not go through the land of Samaria on their way from Galilee to Judea. They actually circumvented this territory so they would not meet Samaritans on the way.

However, Jesus was a different sort of Jew. He was in no way prejudiced. He had come to die for the world—not just for Jews. Jesus told this woman that she too could inherit eternal life, even though she was not a Jew, and in spite of her sin. You see, she had been married five times and she was now involved in an illegitimate relationship (4:17-18).

With this event Jesus was also confronting another prejudice among the Jewish people. Note that when the disciples returned to the well after going to the city to buy food, we read that they "were surprised" to find Jesus "talking with a woman" (4:27). If it was improper for a Jew to come face-to-face with a Samaritan, it was doubly inappropriate for him to associate with a Samaritan woman. Jesus did both, cutting through "the barrier, the dividing wall of hostility." He had come to reconcile both Jew and Gentile "to God by the cross." He preached peace to the Gentiles "who were far away" as well as to the Jews "who were near." Later Paul underscored this very point when he wrote to the Galatians: "There is neither Jew nor Greek, slave nor free, male nor female, for you are all one in Christ Jesus" (Gal. 3:28).

No one then, irrespective of sex, race, color, creed, vocation or social position need feel he or she cannot be a part of God's great plan. Jesus Christ accepts every individual who comes to Him.

The Problem of Pride

As we've seen, prejudice and its reflection through pride has been a problem even among the people God chose to represent Him on earth. What about you and me?

As I reflect on my own background, I can see how prejudiced I had become because of what I had been taught from childhood. I'd grown up in a restrictive and legalistic religious community. In retrospect I can also see part of that prejudice was ethnic. For years I had been taught that I was better than other people because of my heritage. All other people who called themselves "Christian" were wrong. I had the truth. No one else did.

Though I rejected those attitudes after I became a true Christian, I did not realize at first how ingrained they were in me. Those prejudiced feelings lingered in my heart. I can see now that God used some very disillusioning experiences in my life to help me break out of my narrow, provincial and subtle prejudice. In fact, it was only as I was "reaching up to touch bottom" in my spiritual and emotional life that I truly realized how much I needed other people who were not from my own religious and ethnic background.

We must deal with prejudice and pride if we are going to be true to God's Word and walk in His will. All of us struggle with this problem at some level in our own personalities.

We must realize that it is only by God's grace that we are what we are. Truly, "God does not show favoritism" (Acts 10:34), and neither should we (Jas. 2:1).

SOME QUESTIONS TO THINK ABOUT

Are you able to accept other people for who they are?

Do you see the best in people?

Do you freely associate with people who are different from you?

If you can answer yes to these questions, you are no doubt relatively free from prejudice in your Christian life.

SUGGESTION: Think of one person whom you have difficulty liking because he or she is different from you. Seek out that one person and love him/her as Christ loved you.

10

Understanding
Our Mission In Life

EPHESIANS 3:1,13

For this reason I, Paul, the prisoner of Christ Jesus for the sake of you Gentiles—

I ask you, therefore, not to be discouraged because of my sufferings for you, which are your glory.

On one occasion I was speaking at a conference in California. While there, my wife Elaine talked with a middle-aged Christian couple who had been on assignment in Red China shortly after this Communist country began to be open for more dialogue and interaction with the Western world. For political reasons this couple was allowed to teach English in one of the universities.

During their stay in Red China, a number of Chinese prisoners were also released, people who had been incarcerated because they were a threat to Communist ideology. Among them was a pastor, along with some of his congregation. Together they had been in prison for nearly 15 years.

Now free, these believers met together in an old farmyard along with other Christians who congregated to celebrate this glorious day. Looking on, this American couple related the beauty and solemnity of that moment. With eyes filled with tears and hearts filled with joy and praise to God, these people participated in a communion service. This was the first opportunity to remember the Lord in this way for more than a decade.

Reflecting on this eyewitness report regarding this pastor and his little flock, I found it difficult to identify with this experience for obvious reasons. I had never been in prison because of my commitment to Jesus Christ and His message. Few of us in the Western world know anything about persecution, let alone being in prison.

Over the years, however, Christians *have* been imprisoned for their faith, especially those who feel called in a special way to preach the gospel of Christ. And the Apostle Paul stands out as one of the most dynamic New Testament examples. In fact, as he wrote this letter to the Ephesians, he did so from a Roman prison, chained to a Roman guard.

During his first imprisonment, Paul wrote at least four New Testament letters. The first was probably Philippians, followed by Colossians and Philemon. The letter to the Ephesians was no doubt written shortly before he was released for a period of time. He then was imprisoned a second time, which resulted in his martyrdom at the hands of the wicked and notorious Roman emperor, Nero.

In all four of these letters—one of which includes our text

for this chapter—Paul made reference to his prison experience. He also made reference to the reason why he was in prison. That reason? His mission in life.

In the letter to the Philippians Paul said: "Now I want you to know, brothers, that what has happened to me has really served to *advance the gospel*. As a result, it has become clear throughout the whole palace guard and to everyone else that I am in chains for Christ. Because of my chains, most of the brothers in the Lord have been encouraged *to speak the Word of God more courageously and fearlessly*" (Phil. 1:12-14).

In the letter to the Colossians: "Devote yourselves to prayer, being watchful and thankful. And pray for us, too, that God may open a door for *our message,* so that we may *proclaim the mystery of Christ,* for which I am in chains. Pray that I may *proclaim it clearly,* as I should" (Col. 4:2-4).

In the letter to Philemon he stated: "Paul, a prisoner of Christ Jesus, and Timothy our brother, to Philemon our dear friend and fellow worker" (Philem. 1).

And finally, to the Ephesians: "For this reason I, Paul, the prisoner of Christ Jesus *for the sake of you Gentiles* (Eph. 3:1).

THE PRISON SETTING

Paul's first imprisonment is described in the last chapter of the book of Acts. Following a long and very eventful journey, he finally arrived in Rome. Because of the unique circumstances that brought him there (which we'll look at shortly), he was allowed to rent a home and live apart from other prisoners. However, he was chained to a Roman guard 24 hours a day (Acts 28:16).

Three days after he arrived in Rome, Paul "called together the leaders of the Jews" (28:17). He shared with them the events that had brought him there. He also pointed them to the Old Testament Scriptures in order to demonstrate that Jesus Christ was the true Messiah. The response was divided, just as it had been throughout his previous missionary journeys. Some of his fellow Jews responded to the gospel. Others rejected the message.

And once again, after first confronting his own people, he turned to the Gentiles. Thus we read: "For two whole years Paul stayed there in his own rented house and welcomed *all* who came to see him. Boldly and without hindrance *he preached the kingdom of God and taught them about the Lord Jesus Christ* (28:30-31).

THE REASON FOR PAUL'S IMPRISONMENT

When Paul called the leaders of the Jews together in Rome, he said, "It is because of the *hope of Israel* that I am bound with this chain" (Acts 28:20). However, when he wrote to the Ephesians, he said, "I, Paul, the prisoner of Christ Jesus *for the sake of you* Gentiles" (Eph. 3:1).

Are these contradictory explanations? Not at all. Both are true. Israel's hope was focused in the Messiah who was foretold again and again in the Old Testament. But when Jesus Christ came, He made it clear that He had come not only to provide salvation for the Jews but for all people everywhere. And Paul was called to reveal that hope in a special way to the Gentiles. Following Paul's encounter with Jesus Christ on the road to Damascus, the Lord revealed this truth to Ananias, who was initially afraid of this angry Jew who was out to destroy Christians. Consequently, he responded to God's revelation: "I have heard many reports about this man and all the harm he has done to your saints in Jerusalem" (Acts 9:13). However, the Lord responded to Ananias, "Go! This man is my chosen instrument to carry my name *before the Gentiles* and their kings (Acts 9:15).

It was because of Israel's hope that Paul was in prison, but it was also because of Paul's calling to share this message of hope with the Gentiles that he was eventually chained to a Roman guard. Furthermore, it was Paul's ministry to the Gentiles in Ephesus and throughout Asia that eventually brought unusual persecution resulting in his imprisonment. Let's look at those events in more detail.

Paul's Meeting with the Ephesian Elders

In the final stages of Paul's third missionary journey, he

decided to try to reach Jerusalem by the day of Pentecost. Seemingly he had wanted to once again visit the Christians in Ephesus, but changed his plans because of his short time schedule. Consequently, Luke has recorded: "Paul had decided to sail past Ephesus to avoid spending time in the province of Asia, for he was in a hurry to reach Jerusalem, if possible by the day of Pentecost" (Acts 20:16).

But Paul wanted to meet with the spiritual leaders at Ephesus in order to minister to them one final time and to share his deep love and respect for these men. They had become very dear and special to him during his two-year ministry in that city. Consequently, when he arrived in Miletus, he sent a message asking the Ephesian elders to join him there. While spending time together, he relayed to them the following message: "And now, compelled by the Spirit, I am going to Jerusalem, not knowing what will happen to me there. I only know that in every city the Holy Spirit warns me that prison and hardship are facing me. However, I consider my life worth nothing to me, if only I may finish the race and complete the task the Lord Jesus has given me—*the task of testifying to the gospel of God's grace*" (Acts 20:22-24).

That task, of course, involved a target audience—the Gentiles. This was Paul's special mission and calling. Peter was called to minister primarily to the Jews and Paul was called to minister primarily to the Gentiles (Gal. 2:8).

Paul's Experience in Jerusalem

When Paul arrived in Jerusalem, the leaders of the church received him warmly. They were excited about his ministry to the Gentiles. But they were also deeply concerned. Thousands of Jews in Jerusalem had accepted Jesus Christ as the true Messiah, but they were still "zealous for the law"—especially believing that the rite of circumcision was to be a necessary part of their religious experience.

The "dividing wall of hostility" Paul had written about in his Ephesian letter still existed in the minds of these people (Eph. 2:14). They deeply resented the Gentiles who had professed faith in Christ. Furthermore, they resented Paul for leading these people to Christ and teaching them that it was no longer necessary to keep the ritualistic laws of Israel.

Interestingly, it was a group of Jews from the province of Asia who stirred up the Jewish Christians in Jerusalem (Acts 21:27). No doubt they had heard Paul teach in the lecture hall of Tyrannus in Ephesus. For two years, you'll remember, Paul had continued this ministry on a daily basis. As a result of this effort, Luke has recorded "that all the Jews and Greeks who lived in the province of Asia heard the Word of the Lord" (19:10).

It was some of these Jews who precipitated the riot against Paul in Jerusalem. One of their accusations was that Paul had brought "Trophimus the *Ephesian*" into the Temple area and had defiled their holy place. Thus, we can understand more fully why Paul wrote to the Ephesians saying, "I, Paul, the prisoner of Christ Jesus for the sake of you Gentiles . . . " (Eph. 3:1). You can also understand more clearly why he later said, "I ask you, therefore, not to be discouraged because of my sufferings for you, which are your glory" (3:13). The beginning of Paul's problems in Jerusalem were directly related to Asian Jews who had heard him speak in Ephesus. Furthermore, it was a Gentile Christian from Ephesus who was used as evidence against Paul, even though Luke records that there was no evidence that Trophimus had actually gone into the Temple area.

What resulted in Jerusalem was no minor complaint session. "The whole city was aroused, and the people came running from all directions" (Acts 21:30). They seized Paul and tried "to kill him" (21:31). If Roman soldiers had not stepped in, they would have beaten him to death.

Paul was taken into custody. Bound in chains, he asked to speak to his accusers. Granted permission, he addressed his fellow Jews, sharing with them his own efforts to persecute Christians and how he had been converted to Jesus Christ on the road to Damascus. The crowd listened attentively to his testimony— *until* he reported that the Lord had told him, "Go; I will send you far away to the *Gentiles* (22:21). The very name "Gentile" once again ignited their anger. "They raised their voices and shouted, 'Rid the earth of him! He's not fit to live'" (22:22).

Paul's Journey to Rome

Once again we can understand more clearly Paul's statement to the Ephesians: "I, Paul, the prisoner of Jesus Christ for the sake of you Gentiles . . . " (Eph. 3:1). The riots and acts of persecution against him in Jerusalem eventually resulted in his imprisonment in Rome. He was miraculously protected from an assassination attempt in Jerusalem and was transferred to Caesarea.

Appearing before several Gentile magistrates, he was eventually sent to Rome to stand before Caesar. And during the two-year waiting period, staying in his own rented quarters, chained to a Roman guard, Paul continued his ministry of teaching and writing. It was during that time that he wrote to the Ephesian Christians, encouraging them not to be discouraged because of his sufferings for them. Paul understood that this was a part of his great spiritual calling and he had no regrets. He would gladly do everything all over again in order to be faithful to the task that God had given him.

Most Bible expositors agree that Paul was eventually acquitted and set free. His prayers were answered, enabling him to return to Philippi, Colossae and Ephesus—perhaps to fellowship with the elders he thought he would never see again. In fact, some believe he was arrested again *in Ephesus*. This time he was treated like a common criminal. It was then he penned his final letter. Writing to Timothy he said, "I am suffering even to the point of being chained like a criminal" (2 Tim. 2:9).

Facing the reality of death, Paul penned these incredible words: "For I am already being poured out like a drink offering, and the time has come for my departure. I have fought the good fight, I have finished the race, I have kept the faith. Now there is in store for me the crown of righteousness" (2 Tim. 4:6-8).

Those were difficult days for Paul. Many of his friends forsook him. He reported that at his first defense no one came to his support (4:16). "But," Paul wrote with a faith that would not die, "the Lord stood at my side and gave me strength, so that through me the message might be fully proclaimed and *all the Gentiles might hear it*" (4:17).

Tradition tells us that Paul was a martyr. He died by decapitation. Clement reports that "weeping friends took up his corpse and carried it for burial to those subterranean labyrinths where, through many ages of oppression, the persecuted church found refuge for the living, and sepulchers for the dead" (Clement, Rom. 1:5).[1]

WHAT IS *YOUR* MISSION IN LIFE?

Paul had a mission and no matter the obstacles, threats or the degree of persecution, he was never deterred from what he felt was God's will for his life. Nothing turned him aside. Specifically, that mission was to carry the gospel to the Gentiles.

We, too, have a mission. Though Paul's calling was unique, we too have a calling. Paul made that mission and calling clear when he wrote to the Ephesians and said, "Live as children of light (for the fruit of the light consists in all goodness, righteousness and truth), and find out what pleases the Lord. Have nothing to do with the fruitless deeds of darkness, but rather expose them" (Eph. 5:8-11).

- How committed are you to this mission?
- To what extent does it occupy your thinking, no matter what your vocation in life?
- How is this mission reflected in your priorities?

I was rather encouraged with an experience my son Kenton had when he graduated from high school. Since he loves to ski, he had been thinking for some time about attending a summer ski camp to develop his racing skills. Though he's done a lot of superb skiing on all kinds of slopes, he had never had intense training in slalom and giant slalom skiing. Since it was a dream of his at least to test his abilities and skills to see if he could qualify for competitive skiing, his mother and I encouraged him. And so he entered the nine-day Bob Beattie Racing School at Mount Bachelor in Oregon. There were 30 students enrolled.

The first night he called he shared with us that he had entered a whole new world in terms of life-style. First of all, Kenton was the youngest guy enrolled. And after the students left the slopes and ate dinner, most of them hit the bars and picked up girls, married men included. The very first day he was exposed to a new dimension of the world's values.

Nevertheless, things went well for Kenton. He made a lot of progress through the week, got good positive feedback from his coaches and was generally encouraged. One evening toward the end of his time at camp, he called and told us that he planned to meet with one of his coaches later that evening to discuss his potential future as a competitive skier. Elaine and I assured him of our prayers and the next morning he called bright and early. Hearing his excited voice on the other end of the line, I thought for sure I was going to get a positive report on his talk with the coach.

"Hey, Dad," he said. "I got to talking with this guy last night in the Jacuzzi. He's really searching spiritually and asked me some real heavy questions about Christianity. I need some help."

Kenton then began to unload all these "heavies" on me, seeking answers. While I was trying to answer his questions, another question kept intruding on my mind. I was wondering what the coach had said last night.

Finally, when we had ended our conversation on spiritual issues, I asked him about his conference with his coach. "How did it go?" I queried.

"Oh, okay, Dad!" he said. "But I have to go now. I'm running late. Talk to you later. Good-bye."

After I hung up, I got to thinking about that conversation. Though I was somewhat disappointed that I didn't hear about his time with his coach I began to see our conversation in a different light. My disappointment turned to thanksgiving for Kenton's concern for a guy who needed Christ. In fact, my thoughts went back to an earlier conversation that Kenton and I had had before he ever left for camp. He was trying to evaluate his motives for wanting to ski competitively. As he concluded the conversation, he stated clearly that he felt that his primary desire was to glorify God with any opportunities that might come his way.

As I reflected on our telephone conversation, I realized that he was attempting to keep his priorities straight. As his dad, I was thrilled as I reflected, but I was also somewhat convicted about my own attitudes. I was initially more concerned about his coach's report than his witnessing experience. I'm well aware that initial reactions are quite revealing regarding our real motives.

Several days later Elaine and I met Kenton at the airport. Again we were anxiously waiting to hear the full story of his progress. He still hadn't given one. After all, we footed the bill! We were entitled to a report.

He got off the plane and after he had greeted us and his girlfriend warmly, he asked a question immediately.

"Did you hear from Jim?" he asked. Jim was the guy he had discussed Christ with. "I bought a copy of C. S. Lewis's *Mere Christianity* in Seattle," he continued, "and mailed it to him. I think there is a real possibility that this guy could become a Christian."

I stood listening and thinking! Once again, my mind was on his progress as a skier. His mind was on the guy he had witnessed to. And again, I had learned a lesson. Oftentimes we are so concerned about the legitimate and important things in life that we forget those things that are *most* important. My real concern now is that he will maintain those priorities that I saw demonstrated that week.

Incidentally, the coach's report was very encouraging. In fact, he sent Kenton a list of possible places he could go to continue his training to ski competitively. However, after a lot of soul-searching regarding his future vocational goals, Kenton made a tough decision. He decided to enter Baylor University, following in his two sisters' footsteps. To this day, he has not regretted this decision. But he is happy he had the opportunity at least to test his skills—with positive feedback.

A PERSONAL THOUGHT

Our mission in life determines our decisions and actions. Before asking ourselves if we'd really go to prison for Christ's sake, perhaps we ought to ask ourselves if we are putting Christ ahead of the other important things in our lives.

It is true that God has given us all talents and responsibilities. Your talent may be in the area of homemaking and mothering. However, are you using those talents to achieve the really important goals in life—to be a light for Jesus Christ in this world? Your talent may be making money. However, are you using that talent to advance the cause of Christ? Your talent may be in the area of music or in speaking. How are you using those talents to carry out the will of God?

Whatever your talents, don't bury them and don't use them primarily for yourself. Use them to advance the kingdom of God. If you do, you'll be true to the mission that God has for all of us (Matt. 25:14-30).

Note

1. From *Unger's Bible Dictionary,* by Merrill F. Unger, Copyright 1957, 1961, 1966 by Moody Press. Moody Bible Institute of Chicago. Used by permission.

11

Responding To
God's Great Mystery

EPHESIANS 3:2-12

Surely you have heard about the administration of God's grace that was given to me for you, that is, the mystery made known to me by revelation, as I have already written briefly. In reading this, then, you will be able to understand my insight into the mystery of Christ, which was not made known to men in other generations as it has now been revealed by the Spirit to God's holy apostles and prophets. This mystery is that through the gospel the Gentiles are heirs together with Israel, members together of one body, and sharers together in the promise in Christ Jesus.

I became a servant of this gospel by the gift of God's grace given me through the working of his power. Although I am less than the least of all God's people, this grace was given me: to preach to the Gentiles the unsearchable riches of Christ, and to make plain to everyone the administration of this mystery, which for ages past was kept hidden in God, who created all things. His intent was that now, through the church, the manifold wisdom of God should be made known to the rulers and authorities in the heavenly realms, according to his eternal purpose which he accomplished in Christ Jesus our Lord. In him and through faith in him we may approach God with freedom and confidence.

All of us as parents have been faced with the task of unveiling the mystery of life. I remember when my two daughters were about four and five years old. I was home one evening with them while Elaine, my wife, was out. My girls wanted me to read to them, something we did frequently when they were small.

So, I thought I would take advantage of this "teachable moment" and read from the New Testament. I picked up a copy of *Good News for Modern Man,* a contemporary English translation, and began to read the story of Jesus' birth in chapter 1 of the Gospel of Matthew.

They sat quietly, taking it all in, until I read verses 22 and 23: "Now all this happened in order to make come true what the Lord had said through the prophet, 'A virgin will become pregnant and have a son.' . . . So when Joseph woke up he married Mary, as the angel of the Lord had told him to. But he had no sexual relations with her before she gave birth to her son. And Joseph named him Jesus" (Matt. 1:22-23,25, *TEV*).

I could sense as I was reading, both from the context in this passage and the twinkle in their eyes, that I was headed for an interrogation session. Four- and five-year-olds, of course, are filled with questions anyway.

My perceptions were right. Suddenly, two quiet little girls pounced on their daddy like chickens on a June bug. This was their golden opportunity to ask some personal questions that had been emerging in their young minds. "Daddy," one said, "what is a virgin?" "Daddy," the other one said, "what does 'pregnant' mean?" "Daddy," they asked, "what are sexual relations?"

Somehow, I sensed that this was the moment that they had been waiting for. I think they felt more encouraged because these were words that were used in the Bible. I must admit that I was not exactly prepared mentally or psychologically to face this sudden and unexpected turn of events. But what a golden opportunity to explain the mystery of life!

So often these questions surface in children's minds because of what they have heard from other children and in a context and environment that is anything but edifying. Usually they pool their ignorance based upon knowledge that has been passed on from other children who have anything but an adequate view of what sexuality is all about. What better context could I have asked for to discuss the mystery of life than the story of the birth of Jesus Christ, the One who created life in the first place?

The birth process is indeed a great and wonderful mystery. Even in his day, David understood this reality, which he expressed in Psalm 139: "For you created my inmost being; you knit me together in my mother's womb. I praise you because I am fearfully and wonderfully made; your works are wonderful, I know that full well." (Ps. 139:13-14).

Today, through the efforts of medical science, we know even more than David did. The miracle of conception boggles the mind. And yet with all our knowledge, it remains a mystery that can only be partially understood. Yet we know it is true. And the more this mystery is unveiled, the more amazing it appears.

The mystery of life *is* awesome and wonderful, but more so is the mystery of *eternal life*. And this is the subject developed by Paul in the next section of his letter to the Ephesians. Four times he used the word "mystery" (3:3,4,6,9), a mystery that was unveiled to him in a special way. In essence he was talking about the mystery of eternal life, but with a particular focus.

THE MYSTERY DEFINED

Paul defined this mystery in a threefold way in verse 6. He wrote: "This mystery is that through the gospel the Gentiles are:
- *heirs together* with Israel,
- *members together* of one body, and
- *sharers together* in the promise of Jesus Christ" (Eph. 3:6).

To be "heirs together" means that all men and women, whether Jews or Gentiles, can share in the same inheritance. Thus Paul wrote to the Galatians: "There is neither Jew nor Greek, slave nor free, male nor female, for you are *all one* in Christ Jesus. If you belong to Christ, then you are Abraham's seed, and *heirs* according to the promise" (Gal. 3:28-29).

God's promise to Abraham, hundreds of years before Christ came (Gen. 12:1-3), included not only the Jews but also the

Gentiles. We are "heirs together" in God's eternal kingdom.

To be "members together of one body" is not only a "positional" truth but a reality that is practical and functional. Paul used the word *sunsoma* to express this concept. As far as we know, this word was never used before in the Greek language. Some believe Paul coined the term to explain this marvelous mystery. Evidently he could find no word or words rich enough in meaning to describe the meaning of it all.

This concept is functional. Not only are all people who put their faith in Christ "heirs together in God's eternal kingdom," but we are "members together" in the here and now. The Church of Jesus Christ is a present reality. Every believer is a significant part of the Church, just as every member of our physical body is a significant part of the whole. Thus Paul wrote to the Roman Christians, first using an analogy of the human body and then applying that analogy to the Church:

The analogy: "Just as each of us has *one body* with many members, and these members do not all have the same function . . . " (Rom. 12:4).

The application of the analogy: "So in Christ we who are many form *one body,* and each member belongs to all the others" (12:5).

To be "sharers together" involves both realities; that is, we all share in our eternal inheritance and we all share in each other's lives in the here and now. There will be no barriers in heaven, and there should be no barriers among Christians on earth.

John Wesley once dreamed that he was at the gates of hell. He knocked and asked, "Are there any Roman Catholics here?"

"Yes, many," was the reply.

"Any Church of England men?"

"Yes, many."

"Any Presbyterians?"

"Yes, many."

"Any Wesleyans here?"

"Yes, many."

Disappointed and dismayed, especially at the last reply, Wesley turned his steps upward and found himself at the gates of heaven. Here he repeated the same questions. Finally, he asked—"Are there any Wesleyans here?"

"No," came the reply.

"Whom have you here, then?" he asked in astonishment.

"We do not know of any here which you have named. The only name of which we know anything is 'Christian.'"

Thus Paul wrote earlier in the Ephesian letter: "For he himself is our peace, who has made the two one and has destroyed the barrier, the dividing wall of hostility, by abolishing in his flesh the law with its commandments and regulations. His purpose was to create in himself one new man out of the two, thus making peace, and in this one body to reconcile both of them to God through the cross, by which he put to death their hostility" (Eph. 2:14-16).

THE MYSTERY REVEALED

To Paul

This marvelous mystery regarding the hope of eternal life for all who believe in Jesus Christ was unveiled to Paul in a special way. "Surely you have heard about the administration of God's grace that was given to me for you," he wrote; "that is, the mystery *made known to me by revelation,* as I have already written briefly" (3:2-3).

Paul received his "insight into the mystery of Christ" (3:4) by special revelation. This means that God spoke to him directly. This process began on the Damascus Road, resulting in his conversion to Jesus Christ (Acts 9:3-6). The process continued for the next several years, and when Paul wrote to the Galatians he explained this experience in more detail: "I want you to know, brothers, that the gospel I preached is not something that man made up. I did not receive it from any man, nor was I taught it; rather, I received it by revelation from Jesus Christ" (Gal. 1:11-12).

Following Paul's conversion, he did not consult others. He didn't even go back to Jerusalem for at least three years. Rather, after having to leave Damascus because of persecution, he went into Arabia. Here, evidently in semi-isolation from those who knew him, he had direct communication from God regarding his unique calling to preach the gospel to the Gentiles (Gal. 1:13-17).

Then, "after three years," Paul "went up to Jerusalem to get acquainted with Peter." He stayed there only 15 days (1:18), and evidently did not return to Jerusalem for 14 years. All this time (about 17 years following his conversion) he had not met with the other apostles. This time he returned with his friend Barnabas and met all of the apostles (2:1-3).

It is rather startling that after all this time the disciples in Judea were still "all afraid of him." They were not convinced he was really a believer. But his friend Barnabas knew firsthand what had happened to this man. Having unusual credibility with the apostles, Barnabas arranged an audience with them, taking Paul with him. He shared with them that Saul, no doubt 17 years earlier, "had seen the Lord and that the Lord had spoken to him, and how in Damascus he had preached fearlessly in the name of Jesus" (Acts 9:27). His ministry in Damascus evidently involved his initial ministry following his conversion (9:19-25) and his later ministry when he returned from Arabia (Gal. 1:17).

It is important to note that his visit to Jerusalem with Barnabas was the result of a direct revelation from God. All this time the Lord must have been periodically communicating with Paul regarding his special calling to preach the gospel to the Gentiles (Gal. 2:2).

To the Apostles

This mystery was not only revealed to Paul. It was also revealed to the other "apostles and prophets" (Eph. 3:5). God spoke to Paul first. Then three years later, Paul shared his experience with Peter. Fourteen years later, he shared it with *all* the apostles. And then, God spoke directly to Peter. It began with a vision on a housetop and was verified through Peter when he saw Cornelius and his whole household come to Christ (Acts 10:1-48).

This is a very important observation. God was not satisfied to reveal this mystery to only one man. He also revealed it directly to Peter and then to the other apostles and prophets.

This was necessary to verify to the world that this message was true.

How different from those who have claimed to have revelations in recent years, those who have started their own religions. Mormonism was started by one man, Joseph Smith. His so-called "revelations" were never verified by others. And yet, millions of people follow the teachings of this man which are embodied in the *Book of Mormon*.

False religions grow out of so-called "revelations" that are "made known" to one person and are nonverifiable. On the other hand, God's true revelations are always revealed to more than one person, and those revelations are always consistent and in harmony.

Note one other important observation. True revelation is always in harmony with previous revelations. This point of verification is dramatically illustrated during the Jerusalem council, when all of the believers met to resolve the theological conflict between the believing Jews who mixed law and grace and the believing Jews who understood the pure gospel of the grace of God. There were several significant steps taken in this council meeting.

- *First,* Paul and Barnabas reported that Gentiles had been saved as a result of the ministry (Acts 15:4).
- *Second,* Peter reported his experience of seeing Cornelius and his family come to Christ.
- *Third,* James reported that what Paul and Barnabas and Peter had reported as being true was *in harmony* with what God had already revealed through the prophets in the Old Testament (15:15-18).

One final point. Hardly without exception, God's direct revelations are also verified with signs and wonders and miracles. When God speaks to mankind directly, He wants people to know it is His voice. He does not communicate secretively.

THE MYSTERY COMMUNICATED

We've already observed that Paul had a special calling in receiving knowledge of this mystery directly from God. It follows naturally that he also had a special responsibility to communicate this message. Thus he wrote: "I became a servant of this gospel by the gift of God's grace through the working of his power" (Eph. 3:7).

Paul never got over the grace of God in calling him to this great task. He truly considered himself "less than the least of all God's people" (3:8). In his blindness he had persecuted Christians. He was proud and arrogant in his ignorance. Yet God called *him* "to preach to the Gentiles the unsearchable riches of Christ" (3:8). God called *him* "to make plain to everyone the administration of this mystery, which for ages past was kept hidden in God, who created all things" (3:9).

Paul was indeed humbled to receive God's mercy. It is no wonder that this apostle felt such an indebtedness to both Greeks and non-Greeks, making known to them the gospel of Jesus Christ (Rom. 1:14-15). And as we've seen, he was true to this eternal calling until the day his head was severed from his body at the hands of a wicked Roman emperor. And because of Paul's commitment to preaching the gospel, millions of us who know Christ today have this knowledge and this personal experience of salvation. Paul and most of the other apostles literally gave their lives that we might know about this marvelous mystery.

What is so amazing is that our calling today involves not only communicating this same message to the others around the world, but God has called us to reveal this message to "the rulers and authorities in the heavenly realms" (Eph. 3:10). This helps us understand more clearly why the message of the gospel was identified by Paul as a "mystery." Even the angels of heaven did not understand God's eternal purpose before it actually happened in time and space.

The reality of God's Church, made up of people from all walks of life and from all nationalities was a startling revelation to those eternal spirits who have inhabited eternity. And so Paul says that, because of this great reality, all of us who know Jesus Christ "may approach God with freedom and confidence" (3:12). We can approach His throne of grace at any moment and at any time. Jesus Christ is our great High Priest, our Mediator, our Intercessor.

GOD'S MYSTERY AND YOU

How should a Christian respond to these great realities, particularly to Paul's personal experience? Though our calling and responsibilities are certainly different from Paul's, our heart response should be the same.

We Should Respond with Humility

Paul never got over the fact that God's Spirit touched his life in spite of who he was and what he had been doing to Christians. As he wrote to the Philippians, he was a proud and arrogantly religious man. "If anyone else thinks he has reasons to put confidence in the flesh," he wrote, "I have more:

• circumcised on the eighth day,
• of the people of Israel,
• of the tribe of Benjamin,
• a Hebrew of Hebrews;
• in regard to the law, a Pharisee;
• as for zeal, persecuting the church;
• as for legalistic righteousness, faultless" (Phil. 3:4-6).

But when God had mercy on Paul in the midst of his pride, anger and resentment, he was overwhelmed with God's grace. The Lord had built into his personality a humility that pervaded his character all his life. He truly believed that he was "less than the least of all God's people (Eph. 3:8).

Don't misunderstand. His self-confidence was not destroyed. His boldness was not eliminated. His zeal was not eradicated. Rather, all of these things were redirected, but now through a man whose ultimate confidence was in the Lord Jesus Christ, not in himself.

Some Christians become confused at this point. They interpret meekness as weakness; humility as being withdrawn and inactive. Not at all! In fact, many of our personality traits will remain the same but are now devoted to doing God's will, not our own. Thus it was with Paul.

As Multnomah's John Mitchell has stated, mankind's truly great leaders have always been servants. True nobility is manifest by those who serve, not by the arrogant and the avaricious.

And the greatest servant of all? The Son of God Himself, who "did not come to be served, but to serve, and to give his life as a ransom for many" (Mark 10:45).

Many years ago John Newton lay upon his death bed. Before he was converted to Jesus Christ he had been a slave trader and had lived a very sinful life. After he became a Christian he eventually became a great preacher and poet. As he lay dying, a young clergyman came to see him and expressed deep regret at the prospect of losing so eminent a laborer in the Lord's vineyard.

The venerable servant of the Lord replied, "True, I'm going on before you, but you'll soon come after me. When you arrive, our friendship will no doubt cause you to inquire for me. But I can tell you already where you'll most likely find me—I'll be sitting at the feet of the thief whom Jesus saved in His dying moments on the cross!"

Although Newton was a distinguished man, he felt with Paul that he could only classify himself among the chief of sinners who have been saved through marvelous grace. That is *true* humility.

We Should Respond with Indebtedness

Paul was indebted to Jesus Christ the rest of his life, not because of guilt, but because of appreciation and love. He devoted himself to fulfilling his heavenly calling and explaining the mystery of the gospel that had been revealed to him.

We, too, should respond to God's mercy and grace in saving us. This was Paul's message in Romans 12:1-2: "Therefore," he wrote, "I urge you, brothers, *in view of God's mercy,* to offer *your bodies* as living sacrifices, holy and pleasing to God—which is your spiritual worship." Can we do less than give ourselves to God when He has given His only Son for us?

Perhaps no person on the contemporary scene illustrates indebtedness more than Chuck Colson. He was a tough, arrogant politician. Pride and ego dominated his life. Wonderfully and marvelously he was converted to Jesus Christ during the Watergate scandal. And while serving a prison term for his crime, he began to mature in Jesus Christ. Later he wrote a book entitled *Born Again,* which is a moving and gripping story of what God did in his life.

The sequel to that book is *Life Sentence,* a very descriptive title. While in prison, Chuck Colson developed a tremendous burden to see prisoners find life in Jesus Christ and to also see prisons reformed in order to better help those downtrodden individuals. Consequently, he felt led to devote his life to this task. Hence the title of his second book: *Life Sentence*! Overwhelmed at God's mercy in his own life, he decided to become a "prisoner for Jesus Christ" to help these forgotten people.

Chuck Colson openly declared his "life sentence" one evening while speaking to a thousand inmates in a sweltering Atlanta prison. It was a very tense and fearful situation. The crowd was unpredictable.

It was in this setting that Chuck laid aside his prepared speech and shared the following message:

> Jesus Christ came into this world for the poor, the sick, the hungry, the homeless, the imprisoned. He is the Prophet of the loser. And all of us are losers. I am a loser just like every one of you. The miracle is that God's message is specifically for those of us who have failed.

And then at the end of the message, Chuck Colson declared his own life sentence:

> Jesus, the Saviour, the Messiah, the Jesus Christ I follow is the one who comes to help the downtrodden and the oppressed and to release them and to set them free. This is the Jesus Christ to whom I've committed my life. This is the Jesus Christ to whom I have offered up my dream and said, "Lord, I want to help these men because I have lived among them. I came to know them, I love them. There is injustice in our society, but we can change it. Yes, God, we can change it. *I give my life to it* (italics added)."[1]

All of us as Christians can show our indebtedness to Jesus Christ in various ways. Paul fulfilled his calling in the first century. And Chuck Colson is fulfilling his in the twentieth.

WHAT ABOUT YOU?

Are you expressing your indebtedness to Jesus Christ in your own set of circumstances? You can! The place to begin is with Romans 12:1. In view of His mercy, give yourself to Jesus Christ unreservedly and without conditions. And then you'll discover the specific ways you can demonstrate your love for Jesus Christ and your indebtedness to Him in your home, on the job, at school, in your church and in the other circumstances of life.

Notes

1. Taken from LIFE SENTENCE, by Charles W. Colson. Copyright © 1979 by Charles Colson. Used by permission of Zondervan Pubishing House.

Looking Up
Through Prayer

EPHESIANS 3:14-21

For this reason I kneel before the Father, from whom his whole family in heaven and on earth derives its name. I pray that out of his glorious riches he may strengthen you with power through his Spirit in your inner being, so that Christ may dwell in your hearts through faith. And I pray that you, being rooted and established in love, may have power, together with all the saints, to grasp how wide and long and high and deep is the love of Christ, and to know this love that surpasses knowledge—that you may be filled to the measure of all the fullness of God.

Now to him who is able to do immeasurably more than all we ask or imagine, according to his power that is at work within us, to him be glory in the church and in Christ Jesus throughout all generations, for ever and ever! Amen.

What do you and I as true born-again believers have in Jesus Christ? Someone has stated that we have:

- A love that can never be fathomed
- A life that can never die
- A righteousness that can never be tarnished
- A peace that can never be understood
- A rest that can never be disturbed
- A joy that can never be diminished
- A hope that can never be disappointed
- A glory that can never be clouded
- A light that can never be darkened
- A happiness that can never be interrupted
- A strength that can never be enfeebled
- A purity that can never be defiled
- A beauty that can never be marred
- A wisdom that can never be baffled
- Resources that can never be exhausted.

In many respects this is what Paul was communicating to the followers of Jesus Christ in his Ephesian letter. Some of these things are guaranteed by virtue of our personal relationship with Christ, such as God's unconditional love, a hope that will never fade, a righteousness that goes on forever. Many of these things, however, are potentially ours if we choose to grow and mature in our relationship with God and take advantage of the divine resources available to us.

PAUL'S PRAYER AT A GLANCE

Paul makes clear what we have in Jesus Christ in his prayer for the Ephesians. In many respects it is a model prayer for Christians to pray for others and for Christians to pray for themselves both corporately and as individuals.

What appears to be two prayers in this Epistle is actually one prayer. In fact, this single prayer in many respects forms the grammatical framework upon which Paul builds his thoughts and ideas, beginning in verse 15 of chapter 1. This becomes very clear when these two prayer segments are put together, as illustrated in the grammatical layout in figure 2.

In this layout in figure 2, note the phrase "for this reason." Paul used this basic concept three times to set the stage for his prayer (Eph. 1:15; 3:1,14). The first time he used the phrase (1:15) he had just stated *why* ("the reason") he was going to pray for these believers. They had been "included in Christ" when they "heard the word of truth" (1:13), had become Christians and received the Holy Spirit. And because this was true—"for this reason"—Paul asked God to help them to grow and mature in their Christian lives.

Paul began by asking God for three things:

- That they might receive the Spirit of wisdom and revelation so that they *may know God better* (1:17).
- That the eyes of their hearts may be enlightened so that they may *know the hope* to which God had called them (1:18).
- That they *may also know and comprehend God's great power* demonstrated on their behalf in providing them with eternal salvation (1:19).

At this point in the letter, Paul ceased praying and began explaining (see fig. 3).

- First, he described God's power by referring to the resurrection of Jesus Christ (1:19-23).
- Second, Paul, in Ephesians 2:1-10, explained God's mercy and grace in making the same power available so that people everywhere "who were dead in transgressions and sins" (2:1), may be "made alive with Christ" (2:5).
- Third, Paul, in a very detailed fashion, outlined that all people, both Jews and Gentiles, who put their faith in Jesus Christ for salvation are then *one in Christ* (2:11-22).

At this point, beginning in Ephesians 3, Paul decided to continue his prayer (see figs. 2 and 3). To establish continuity in the reader's mind, he once again wrote: "For this reason . . . " (3:1), but immediately decided to add a personal testimony regarding his own calling to reveal the wonderful mystery "that through the gospel the Gentiles are heirs together with Israel, members together in one body, and sharers together in the promise in Christ Jesus" (3:6; read 3:2-13).

Finally, Paul continued the prayer he began in chapter 1.

Paul's Prayer at a Glance
Ephesians 1:15-18; 3:14-19

Eph.	**For this reason** (because "you also were included in Christ"—1:13),
1:15	ever since I heard about your faith in the Lord Jesus
	and
	your love for all the saints,
1:16	I have not stopped giving thanks for you,
	remembering you in my prayers.
1:17	I keep asking that the God of our Lord Jesus Christ,
	the glorious Father,
	may give you the Spirit of wisdom **1.**
	and
	revelation,
	so that you may know him better.
1:18	I pray also that the eyes of your heart may be enlightened **2.**
	in order that you may know the hope to which he has called you,
	the riches of his glorious inheritance
	in the saints
	and
1:19	**3.** his incomparably great power
	for us who believe.
3:1	**For this reason** (1:13) (Paul's calling)
	(3:2-13)
3:14	**For this reason** I kneel before the Father,
	from whom his whole family in heaven and on earth derives its name.
3:16	I pray that out of his glorious riches he may strengthen you with power
	through his Spirit **4.**
	in your inner being,
	so that Christ may dwell in your hearts
	through faith.
	And I pray that you, being rooted and established in love,
3:18	may have power, together with all the saints, **5.**
	to grasp how wide and long and high and deep
	is the love of Christ,
	and
3:19	to know this love that surpasses knowledge—
	that you may be filled to the measure
	of all the fullness of God.

Figure 2

Textual Outline

1:13 Because "you also were included in Christ"

1:15 *For This Reason* . . .

> Paul's prayer (1:15-19)
> Paul's explanation of
> • God's Power (1:19-23)
> • God's Grace (2:1-10)
> • Oneness in Christ (2:11-22)

3:1 *For This Reason* . . .

> Paul's explanation of the mystery revealed to him (3:2-13)

3:14 *For This Reason* . . .

> Paul's prayer continued (3:14-19)

> Paul's Doxology (3:20-21)

Figure 3

A Closer Look

Specific Requests	Specific Reasons
1. Give you the Spirit of wisdom and revelation	so that you may know Him better (Eph. 1:17).
2. The eyes of your heart may be enlightened	in order that you may know . . . the hope to which He has called you (1:18).
3. The eyes of your heart may be enlightened	in order that you may know His incomparably great power for us who believe (1:19).
4. Strengthen you with power through His Spirit in your inner being	so that Christ may dwell in your hearts through faith (3:17).
5. Power . . . to grasp . . . the love of Christ, and to know this love that surpasses knowledge	that you may be filled to the measure of all the fulness of God (3:18-19).

Specific Result
To live a life worthy of the calling you have received (4:1).

Figure 4

Once again he established continuity in the minds of the readers by saying, "For this reason . . . " (3:14), that is, because these believers were living proof that Gentiles can be saved. They also, along with Paul and his fellow Jews (1:11) "were included in Christ" and received the Holy Spirit (1:13).

In this final segment of his prayer, Paul included two additional requests, building conceptually on what he had already asked God for on behalf of these believers. He prayed (see fig. 2):

- That they may be strengthened with God's power through His Spirit in their inner being so that Christ may dwell in their hearts through faith (3:16-7).
- That they may be strengthened to grasp and comprehend the greatness of Christ's love and come to know this love that surpasses knowledge, so that they may be filled to the measure of all the fullness of God (3:18-19).

A CLOSER LOOK

Analyzing the content of this prayer more carefully, both in chapter 1 and chapter 3, you will notice five specific *requests* and five specific *reasons* for these requests (see fig. 4). We've already discussed the first three reasons and requests in depth (chaps. 5, 6, 7—"Knowing God Better," "Understanding Our Hope" and "Understanding God's Power"). In essence, Paul was praying that they might come to know God better by knowing more about Him, both intellectually and experientially. The primary means was God's revelation of Himself through Jesus Christ, the living Word of God; the Scriptures, the written Word of God; and the indwelling Holy Spirit who illumines the Christian's mind and heart to understand the will of God through the Word of God.

He was also praying that they might be aware of how secure they are in Jesus Christ and that their hope was based, not on their own effort, but upon the power of God. He wanted them to know that their security and hope was grounded upon the same power that raised Jesus Christ from the dead and seated Him at the right hand of God.

In the second part of Paul's prayer—the primary focus in this chapter—Paul became more specific and more pragmatic. He also became more intense, indicated by the fact that he was praying in a kneeling position (3:14). When Jews prayed they ordinarily *stood* before the Lord. However, when they felt very deeply about the content and object of their prayers, they fell on their knees. This indicates, of course, how deeply Paul, now a Christian, was exercised in his own heart about these believers. He truly wanted them to know and experience the realities of what it means to be a Christian.

Let's look more in depth at his two final requests and the two reasons for these requests (see figure 4).

Specific Requests

"He may strengthen you with power through his Spirit in your inner being (Eph. 3:16). Here Paul was referring both to *external* power and internal power. There is external power of God "which he exerted in Christ when he raised him from the dead and seated him at his right hand in the heavenly realms" (1:20). This is the same power that raised the Ephesian Christians "up with Christ and seated [them] with him" (2:6). Furthermore, this was also the power that God gave the apostles and other selected Christians in the early days of the Church to work mighty miracles in order to bear witness to the fact that the gospel was indeed true (Acts 1:8).

However, Paul was also referring to *internal* power and strength that is released within our hearts and inner beings. This power is rooted in two sources.

First, this power is released when we truly know, understand, and comprehend how secure our position is in Christ (see fig. 2, Eph. 1:17-18; 3:18-19). In this sense, the power is psychological and emotional strength that comes from being *sure* of our position in Christ.

As I reflect on this aspect of Paul's prayer my mind goes back to the time I was a student at Moody Bible Institute in Chicago. This was before I really understood the hope I had in Christ. I was very insecure in my relationship with God. I did not believe I could really know for sure that I was saved.

As students we had the unique opportunity to participate in various ministries in the Chicago area. Many of these opportunities involved Skid Row missions, and there are many in Chicago. I remember how a group of us would get on a street car or bus and head for some of the worst sections of the city. Bars were everywhere; and so were drunken men and women. Some stood around in groups, obviously under the influence of alcohol. Some sat on curbs with their heads between their knees and others were actually out cold, some lying in the gutters. It was a pathetic sight and quite a shock for a young farm boy from Indiana.

When we arrived at a particular mission we would take over the service, lead the singing, share some testimonies and sometimes one of the group would bring a message from the Bible, focusing on how these people could be saved.

Frequently, one of my responsibilities was to share a testimony. But when I stood to share, I felt a horrible fear and sense of anxiety come over me—not because I was afraid of these people, nor was it stage fright. Rather, my fear was rooted in the fact that I could not say for sure that I knew I was a Christian. I had no real assurance in my heart. I felt intensely hypocritical.

For months I struggled with this dilemma until one day I was studying the Scriptures and saw clearly for the first time that I could truly know in an experiential way the hope I had in Christ. The Holy Spirit enlightened my heart to this reality. And when it happened, the fear and uncertainty were gone. I had a new boldness in sharing my faith with others. I had *internal* strength. I was secure in Christ. This, I believe, is—in part at least—what Paul had in mind when he prayed that the Ephesians might be strengthened in their *inner being.*

The second source of internal power relates directly to God's indwelling Spirit. However, it is clear from Paul's prayer that this power is intrinsically related to knowledge and truth. The power of God's Spirit is released in our lives through our experiential interaction with both the written Word (Scripture) and the living Word (Jesus Christ). And this leads to a specific reason for this request.

Specific Reason

"So that Christ may dwell in your hearts by faith" (Eph. 3:17). Jesus Christ was no longer visible when Paul wrote to the Ephesians. Nevertheless, He was alive, and through His Spirit He was living within their hearts.

To accept this reality involves faith. To be vital, faith must be based on facts, even though these facts reflect invisible realities. The author of the book of Hebrews stated that "faith is being sure of what we hope for and certain of what we do not see" (Heb. 11:1).

The apostles and many other New Testament Christians saw Christ. They walked with Him, touched Him and lived with Him. They saw Him die, and more important, they saw the undeniable evidence that He was indeed raised from the dead. They heard Him speak of His return and then saw Him ascend to heaven.

Paul too saw Christ, but miraculously so. This was a privilege afforded very few people after the Lord Jesus returned to heaven. The Ephesian Christians could only respond to what they *heard* about Christ. True, in the early days of the Church, God bore witness to the message of Christ and salvation "by signs, wonders and various miracles and gifts of the Holy Spirit" (Heb. 2:4). The Ephesians saw many of these "extraordinary miracles" (Acts 19:11-12).

But the fact remains that Jesus was no longer visible. The temptation, particularly in the midst of persecution and difficulties, would be to grow weary and to waver spiritually. Thus Paul prayed that the Ephesians would have an inner strength through the Word of God and through the ministry of God's Spirit to keep on believing and trusting the living Christ who now lived in their hearts.

Specific Request

"Power . . . to grasp . . . the love of Christ" (Eph. 3:18). To understand and comprehend the extent of Christ's love is a supernatural process. It can only be accomplished by means of God's divine help and power. All the facts in the world cannot help us truly understand it all. In fact, Christ's love "surpasses knowledge." We can spend a lifetime trying to understand the love of God and never plumb its depth. The facts are, we will spend eternity coming to know that love.

A poet tried to capture this reality with the following words:

> The love of God is greater far
> Than tongue or pen can ever tell.
> It goes beyond the highest star,
> And reaches to the lowest hell.
> The guilty pair bowed down with care
> God gave His Son to win.
> His erring child He reconciled,
> And pardoned from his sin.
>
> Could we with ink the ocean fill,
> And were the skies of parchment made,
> Were every stalk on earth a quill,
> And every man a scribe by trade;
> To write the love of God above
> Would drain the ocean dry;
> Nor would the scroll contain the whole,
> Though stretched from sky to sky.
>
> O love of God, how rich and pure!
> How measureless and strong.
> It shall for evermore endure,
> The saints' and angels' song.[1]

Specific Reason

"That you may be filled to the measure of all the fullness of God" (Eph. 3:19). To be filled with God's fullness means, first and foremost, being filled "with the knowledge of God" and "his will" (Col. 1:10-11), of who He is, what He has done for us, and what He desires for our lives. In this sense, Paul is ending his prayer where he began. His first request for these Christians was that they may know God better. To know God better means knowing His love and consequently being filled to all the fullness of God.

Getting to know God better and experiencing His fullness is similar to what God intended to happen in marriage. In fact, in Ephesians 5, Paul used our relationship with Christ as Christians to illustrate the husband/wife relationship.

All of us can remember those moments in our lives when we thought we were in love because of our emotional reactions. We call this infatuation. And, of course, this kind of feeling is not wrong, nor is it necessarily something separate from true love. But the facts are, it is not the basis upon which enduring marriages are built. Married life is *not* one continuing series of emotional highs. True loves sees us through the difficult times as well as the happy times. It does what is right, even when we'd rather not.

The most comprehensive definition of love is found in Paul's letter to the Corinthians. It is paraphrased as follows: "Love is patient and is kind. It does not envy nor does it boast. It is not proud or rude or self-seeking. It is not easily angered, nor does it keep records of wrong. It does not delight in evil, but rejoices in the truth. This kind of love always protects, always trusts, always hopes and always perseveres" (1 Cor. 13:4-7, paraphrased).

This is the kind of stuff quality marriages are made of. And this is the kind of love that endures and grows deeper.

Unfortunately, some Christians have a relationship with God that is built more on infatuation than true love. They rely on emotional highs. They become confused when they don't *feel* good all the time. This, of course, is an unrealistic view of the Christian experience just as it is of marriage.

Furthermore, it can be a very selfish approach to God. Some Christians are always asking, always wanting, always desiring more from God. They want God to make them rich, heal their diseases, give them special gifts, and make them happy and successful. God *does* want to bless us. But to a certain extent this is self-centered love, just as is prevalent in so many marriages. We are not content to get to know God better. We're only concerned about our own needs.

Thus when Paul prayed that these Christians may be "filled to the measure of all the fullness of God," he was not speaking of some ecstatic and supercharged emotional experience. It is true that this kind of knowledge will touch not only our intellect, but also our emotions. This is what leads us to worship God not only with our heads, but also with our hearts. However, God designed a process of getting to know Him that should be ongoing. It should become deeper with each passing day until Christ comes again.

A GRAND DOXOLOGY

Someone has said, "Beware of superlatives. Usually they are used to stretch the truth." However, there is no exaggeration in Paul's concluding statements in his grand doxology. God "*is* able to do *immeasurably* more than all we ask or imagine." The reason is related "to his power that is at work within us" (Eph. 3:20).

In Ephesians 1, Paul spoke of God's *incomparable power* (v. 19). That's true! There is nothing to compare with His omnipotence.

In chapter 3, he spoke of God's *unsearchable riches.* And that too is true. It is no exaggerated comment; no hyperbolic statement to make a point. God's grace and all that that means is unsearchable.

And as Paul concludes this opening section of the letter describing God's power in saving us, keeping us, and encouraging us, he describes the Lord's resources as *immeasurable.*

And we can add another superlative which is certainly implied in this final prayer. God's love is *unfathomable.* It surpasses knowledge. No wonder Paul said, "To him be glory in the church and in Christ Jesus throughout all generations, for ever and ever! Amen" (3:21).

PERSONALIZING PAUL'S PRAYER

The following prayer is based on Paul's prayers for the Ephesians, the Colossians (Col. 1:9-14), and the Philippians (Phil. 1:9-11). Use the following prayer periodically in your own personal time with God:

Glorious Father, please grant me spiritual wisdom and understanding. Fill me with the knowledge of your will so that I may know you better. May my heart be enlightened that I may know the hope to which you have called me; the hope that is based in your grace and love that chose me in Christ Jesus before the creation of the world; the hope that is based on the same power that raised Jesus Christ from the dead and seated Him at your right hand.

I pray that you'll strengthen me with your power through your spirit in my inner being so that Christ may dwell in my heart through faith. May I have power to grasp how wide and long and high and deep Christ's love for me really is. May I know this love that surpasses knowledge so that I may be filled to the measure of the fullness of God.

All this I pray, Father, that I may live a life worthy of you and may please you in every way. As I grow in my knowledge of you, may I bear fruit in every good work. Grant that I may have endurance and patience and joyfully give thanks to you, Father, for my position in Christ.

Note

1. F. M. Lehman, "The Love of God," © 1917, 1945 by Nazarene Publishing House.

THE BIBLICAL RENEWAL SERIES
by
Gene A. Getz

ONE ANOTHER SERIES

Building Up One Another
Encouraging One Another
Loving One Another
Praying for One Another
Serving One Another

PERSONALITY SERIES

Trials and Triumphs (Abraham)
From Prison to Palace (Joseph)
A Man of Prayer (Nehemiah)
Defeat to Victory (Joshua)
When You Feel Like a Failure (David)
When the Pressure's On (Elijah)
When You Feel You Haven't Got It (Moses)

THE MEASURE OF SERIES

Measure of a . . .
Church
Family
Man
Marriage
Woman

BIBLE BOOK SERIES

Pressing on When You'd Rather Turn Back
(Philippians)
Saying No When You'd Rather Say Yes
(Titus)
Believing God When You Are Tempted to Doubt
(James 1)
Doing Your Part When You'd Rather Let God Do It All
(James 2-5)
Looking Up When You Feel Down
(Ephesians 1-3)
Standing Firm When You'd Rather Retreat
(1 Thessalonians)

Sharpening the Focus of the Church presents an overall
perspective for Church Renewal. All of these books are
available from your bookstore.

Some Biblical Renewal Books
from
Regal Books